SPENCER CHRISTIAN'S
WEATHER BOOK

SPENCER CHRISTIAN'S
WEATHER BOOK

SPENCER CHRISTIAN
with Tom Biracree

PRENTICE HALL GENERAL REFERENCE

NEW YORK • LONDON • TORONTO • SYDNEY • TOKYO • SINGAPORE

We wish to thank the following people and organizations for the use of their photographs:

p. viii copyright © 1988 Capital Cities/ABC, Inc.; p. 6 copyright © 1988 Capital Cities/ABC, Inc.; p. 70 Myrtle Beach Area Chamber of Commerce; p. 86 Eric Lantz, Walnut Grove (Minn.) *Tribune*/National Oceanographic and Atmospheric Administration; p. 92 *Associated Press*; p. 120 copyright © 1990 Capital Cities/ABC, Inc.; p. 124 The White House; p. 129 copyright © 1990 Capital Cities/ABC, Inc. All other photos are from the author's collection.

PRENTICE HALL GENERAL REFERENCE
15 Columbus Circle
New York, New York, 10023

PRENTICE HALL and colophon are registered trademarks of
Simon & Schuster Inc.

Library of Congress Cataloging-in-Publication Data
Christian, Spencer.
    Spencer Christian's weather book / Spencer Christian with Tom Biracree
      p.   cm.
    Includes index.
    ISBN 0-671-84746-5
      1. Weather--Popular works.   2. Meteorology--Popular works.
I. Biracree, Tom, 1947-   II. Title.
QC981.2.C47 1993
551.5--dc20   92-42241

Designed by Joel Ponzan, Pink Coyote Designs Inc.

Illustrations by Antonia Felix.

First Edition

This book is dedicated to my parents, Spencer, Sr. and Lucy Christian. They gave me life; and through their love, guidance, and support, they gave meaning to my life.

ACKNOWLEDGMENTS

Doug Hill, my news director at WWBTTV in Richmond, VA. He gave me my first job in television in 1971, and remains a dear friend and constant source of inspiration.

Ron Kershaw, my news director at WBALTV in Baltimore. He taught me more about television in two years than I've learned from anyone else in the business. Ron was brilliant, and it is sad that his life ended while he was still a young man.

Phil Beuth, network executive at Capital Cities/ABC, Inc. who hired me for "Good Morning, America." Phil is a great guy to have as a "boss," because he makes you feel that you're working *with* him, not *for* him.

Tom Biracree and Tony Seidl, without whose assistance this book would not have been possible.

My wife, Diane, and my children, Jason and Jessica, who have been my support team in good times and bad.

I am very thankful for my many blessings.

Spencer Christian

Spencer Christian made this project the most pleasant of all projects. He's living proof that nice guys finish first.

Tony Seidl's enthusiasm got this book off the ground, and his skillful packaging was crucial in its completion period.

Gerry Helferich is the editorial epitome of professionalism and patience under pressure.

Antonia Felix demonstrated the ability to wear a dozen hats, including the brand new one of graphic artist.

Pat Reshen, Joel Ponzan and Alan Blaustein of Pink Coyote Designs, Inc. provided the talent, energy, and passion that turned raw text into a package to be proud of.

Jerry McNiff, the weather wizard of "GMA," contributed his vast knowledge and a few awful jokes.

Finally, my heartfelt appreciation for the encouragement and support from my wife, Nancy, and my son, Ryan, who at age seven is already writing better books than his pop.

Tom Biracree

TABLE OF CONTENTS

Who wouldn't trust the forecast delivered by a man with a face like this?

INTRODUCTION

Everybody talks about the weather, but nobody does anything about it.

I am a weatherman. And, just like everyone else, I talk about the weather. In fact, I get paid for it—it's my job. I study, analyze, and forecast the weather every weekday morning on national television. And yet, just like everyone else, I still can't do anything about it.

Despite my obvious lack of control over the elements, you would be amazed at how often I am held responsible for the weather. People approach me on the street and in all kinds of public (and not so public) places and demand to know "what's wrong with the weather." If there's a dry spell, I can't get through the supermarket checkout line without hearing complaints about brown lawns and withering shrubs. When there's a heat wave, the postman always rings twice just to let me know he's tired of the sweltering weather and wants me to "order" a cold front. And when the mercury plunges below freezing and lingers there, the gas station attendant teases me about not coming back until I have "done something" about the frigid weather.

And it doesn't end there. Can you imagine the wrath I incur when my forecast is inaccurate? I become the Rodney Dangerfield of news reporters—I get no respect! I remember one winter night quite a few years ago, when I worked on a local news program in Richmond, Virginia. My forecast called for partly cloudy skies with cold and windy conditions. Well, Richmond was hit with unexpected snow squalls that night, and the next day an irate viewer called the television station and demanded to speak to "that weather jerk." When I answered the phone, she said she wanted me to come over to her house and "shovel off that six inches of partly cloudy" from her driveway.

Then there was the time, when I worked at a local station in Baltimore, that my 6:00 P.M. forecast called for a chance of flurries. By the time I left the studio to go out to dinner, there were already three or four inches of snow on the ground, and it was still coming down. Knowing that these things happen, of course, I simply shrugged my shoulders and wondered what form of public abuse I would suffer next. It didn't take long for me to find out. As I was seated for dinner at one of my favorite restaurants, I was served a platter with a huge snowball on it—compliments of the house.

When I answered the phone, the lady said she wanted me to come over to her house and "shovel off that six inches of partly cloudy" from her driveway.

It gets worse. Even my own kids give me a hard time when the weather dampens their spirits. When my daughter was in the fourth grade, her class planned a field trip that was "abbreviated" by rain. Actually, it was dumped on...washed out...saturated. That evening, my daughter painted a verbal picture for me of fourteen extremely disappointed youngsters. So the next day, I had to go to her school and explain why I had "let it rain" on their field trip. You can't imagine what a humbling experience that can be—unless you also happen to be a weatherperson.

Let me tell you how I became a weatherman in the first place. It was not really by choice—not by my choice, that is. I began my television career as a news reporter in my hometown area of Richmond, Virginia. As a product of the late sixties student activist generation, I took news very seriously, and I believed it was my mission in life to enlighten the masses, to elevate the collective public consciousness, to save society from its own excesses. My first appearance on the air was in November 1971. After six months on the job, I thought I was on my way to being the journalism giant I had dreamed I would become. But then, the winds of chance began to blow.

One day in the summer of 1972, the man who had been the longtime weatherman at my station resigned very unexpectedly. The news director came to me and asked me to fill in on the weather for a couple of weeks while the station looked for a new weatherperson. I knew a little bit about the jet stream and how the upper level winds tend to guide our weather systems in a generally west-to-east direction, but I certainly was not a meteorologist. I was a journalist—and I had no desire to be "just a weatherman."

During the two weeks that I filled in, I began to feel more comfortable in the new role, so I started to have fun with the weather. I introduced my now infamous puns to the weather presentation, and I began to enjoy the fact that reporting the weather allowed me to project more personality and humor than reporting news. Still, though, I was a serious journalist; and don't you forget it!

At the end of my two-week fill-in stint, the station's general manager called me into his office and said he would like me to become the full-time weatherman. He said my humorous style had caught on with the viewers, and he thought I would be more valuable to the station in the more highly visible role of weatherman than in the more low-profile role of news reporter. Well-l-l, being the serious journalist that I was, I protested, "I'm a newsman." "And I don't do weather," I added with a touch of disdain. "But we could nearly double your salary, if you'd do the weather," he countered. "I'm a weatherman!" I exclaimed. So I traded in some of my late-sixties idealism for a bit of early-seventies capitalism, and the rest is history. And that's what "precipitated" my becoming a weatherman.

It didn't take me long to recognize that weather is of greater concern to a larger number of people daily than perhaps any single news event. Everybody really does talk about the weather, because it affects virtually everything we do. We plan our social events, vacations, how we dress, and work assignments around the weather. Even major military operations are affected by and planned according to the weather. Remember the early days of the air strikes during the Gulf War? Weather was a major factor in the planning of strategy and in the daily briefings. In fact, in my daily weather forecast, I included weather maps of the "theater of war"—by popular demand.

Medical science and modern psychology have also taught us that weather affects our moods. It has been scientifically proven that many people experience wide mood swings with changing weather conditions. Why else do you suppose we use expressions like "sunny disposition" and "stormy temperament"? But that doesn't necessarily mean that sunny days lift our spirits, while rainy days get us down. There are many people who like rainy days—who are more energetic and productive when it's overcast. Some people even find that dark, dreary days make them feel sexier, more sensual.

Whatever the basis of our concern about the weather, and whatever its effect on us may be, one thing is certain—we all have a curiosity about the weather; and that is why I have written this book. I believe it is important that we all have the clearest (no pun intended) understanding of weather that we possibly can. What is a thunderstorm? What causes lightning? How do tornadoes develop? What is the jet stream, and how does it affect our weather? These questions and many more will be answered in my Weather Book.

But you will find much more than just scientific explanations of meteorological phenomena in these pages. I have tried to put a human face on weather. I'll take you with me on my many "weather remotes" and show you what it's like to do a live television broadcast with a hurricane bearing down on you, or in a driving snowstorm producing near-blizzard conditions, or at the top of Mt. Washington, New Hampshire, where winds are routinely clocked at over 150 miles per hour. My broadcasting assignments have taken me to forty-six of the fifty states and into nine foreign countries, so there is certainly a flood of weather stories to tell.

This book also contains a wealth of weather trivia—humorous and amazing facts about weather that I rarely have time to discuss during my two-minute segments on the air. You will travel back in time and learn what a significant role weather has played throughout history. Did you know, for example, that an important Revolutionary War battle was won by the colonists because of the effects of a cold front? Perhaps, after reading this book, you'll give your favorite weatherman—or weatherwoman—a little more respect. (Rodney would appreciate that.)

Once we've finished our historical retrospective, we'll turn our eyes to the future. I'll explain the latest advances in weather forecasting technology and show you why we'll be able to predict dramatic weather events like hurricanes and tornadoes with greater accuracy in the near future. I'll examine our ever-changing climate and answer your questions about global warming and the greenhouse effect. And, finally, I'll help you explore one of the most fascinating and futuristic questions in the scientific community: Will we ever be able to control our weather? Or, to put it differently: will there come a day when we not only talk about the weather, but we can do something about it?

While reading my Weather Book, you will quickly come to realize why everybody talks about the weather—it is an enormously fascinating subject that has a profound effect on our daily lives. Weather is at the same time complex yet easy to understand. It can be fun and exciting, or frightening and destructive. It can elevate our spirits to lofty levels, or drop us into the deepest depressions. Similarly, my Weather Book can serve many functions as well. It can make for enlightening and entertaining reading, while also serving as an important resource book for educational use. I trust that reading this book will be as pleasurable an experience for you as writing it was for me.

A WEATHER HISTORY OF EARTH

Our planet Earth, home to all of us as well as our weather, is a very special place in a huge and violent universe. Although it is relatively young in cosmic terms, the Earth is almost incomprehensibly old to us humans who consider a few thousand years to be a long time. If we represent Earth's history by a 24-hour day, the primates who were our ancestors didn't appear on the scene until 11:59 P.M. All of recorded human history occurred in just one-tenth of a second before midnight.

To understand our weather today—and the weather we're likely to see in the seconds after midnight—we should start by taking a brief look at the history of the Earth's weather and weather makers.

HOW DID EARTH FORM?

Making a star is a messy process. After our sun was born, it was surrounded by a flat ring of leftover particles of gas and dust. As these particles spun around the sun, they frequently collided. Because space was crowded, most of the particles moved so slowly that the collisions were gentle, and the particles clumped together like snowflakes in a blizzard. Over the course of just 100,000 years, space began to clear as some of these bodies grew to be the size of mountains. As their number decreased, their speed increased. In a brutal sort of cosmic demolition derby, they smashed into each other and their numbers grew ever fewer. By random chance, one finally grew so much larger than the others that its gravity caused it to attract the smaller asteroids rapidly. When it reached a diameter of about 500 kilometers, gravitational forces molded it into a spherical shape. This object was the baby Earth, which reached half its present size in about 1 million years.

Over the next 70 million years, the Earth's weather forecast would have read "heavy precipitation"—with the emphasis on "heavy." Falling from the sky was an incredible bombardment of asteroids, impacting at a rate a billion times greater than that at which meteorites enter our atmosphere today. At least once a month Earth was struck by a meteor so large that dust and debris from the collision blotted out all sunlight. The heat generated by

Over the next 70 million years, the Earth's weather forecast would have read "heavy precipitation"—with the emphasis on "heavy."

the impacts was so intense that the entire surface of the planet was a sea of molten lava. If any vacationing aliens had happened to cruise by, they would have seen a planet about as tempting as a vat of molten iron.

HOW DID THE MOON FORM?

Some of the asteroids that formed in the early days of the solar system reached the size of our moon or some of the smaller planets. Very close to 4.5 billion years ago, about 50 million years after the Earth began to form, a giant asteroid the size of Mars plowed into the Earth in a giant impact that sheared off part of the Earth's mantle, destroyed its own mantle, and sent a huge volume of debris into space. Much of this debris fell back to Earth. But a large portion rather quickly clumped together into a body one-fourth the size of Earth, which we call the moon. Within 1,000 years, the moon had formed into a ball still red-hot from the heat of the impact. The moon at this point was so close to Earth that it filled the night sky. Its proximity not only created massive tides, but caused the Earth to rotate faster than it does today—Earth's day was only five hours long. Gradually, tidal forces pushed the

Very close to 4.5 billion years ago, about 50 million years after the Earth began to form, a giant asteroid the size of Mars plowed into the Earth.

Here I am with the Apollo lunar lander at the Smithsonian. The Apollo missions added tremendously to our knowledge of our closest neighbor in space.

moon farther and farther away from the planet. In 100 million years, the moon had traveled half the distance to its present orbit, and the length of Earth's day had doubled to about ten hours.

HOW DID EARTH'S ATMOSPHERE DEVELOP?

Earth's first atmosphere consisted of the hydrogen and helium from which the sun was formed. This mixture sounds highly combustible to us today, but the hydrogen could not ignite—there was no oxygen with which it could combine. Over the course of 10 or 20 million years, this primary atmosphere was soon dissipated. The lighter gases either drifted off into space or were thrown off by the intense bombardment that formed the planet.

The replacement was carbon dioxide that spewed forth from the many volcanos that scarred the young planet. This atmosphere, which was virtually identical to that found on the planet Venus today by space probes, was so thick that the air pressure was about 70 times what it is today. For nearly 2 billion years, the carbon dioxide produced an intense "greenhouse" effect that was instrumental in the development of life on this planet in two ways. First, the atmosphere trapped much more of the heat from a young sun that burned with only 75 percent of the intensity it has today. Without the greenhouse effect, the Earth would have been a frozen world. Even with the atmosphere trapping so much heat, the global temperature was a hardly balmy 52 degrees Fahrenheit, as compared with 59 degrees today. Secondly, the carbon dioxide gradually dissolved in the oceans, producing carbon-based molecules that served as the building blocks of life.

The life that gradually developed in the oceans produced the third-generation atmosphere. The oceans became covered with vast seas of algae and other plants that took in carbon dioxide and gave off oxygen. It took 1.5 billion years before the level of the atmosphere reached 1 percent and another 1.5 billion years before the oxygen level reached the current level of 21 percent. It was only then, about 700 million years ago, that the atmosphere could support life that depended on oxygen.

The oceans became covered with vast seas of algae and other plants that took in carbon dioxide and gave off oxygen.

WHICH WAY TO THE BEACH?— THE FORMATION OF LAND

The Earth, like an apple, has three basic layers. The *core* consists of a solid iron ball 500 miles thick, which floats in a sack of molten iron 1,600 miles thick. The *mantle* is an 1,800-mile thick region of rock that ranges in density from fiery liquid to a plastic-like consistency. The *crust*, which in relation to the rest of the Earth is thinner than the skin of an apple, ranges from five to 25 miles thick. The crust isn't made up of one solid piece, but rather a number of gigantic plates that float on the mantle like blocks of wood in a bathtub.

In the Earth's earliest days, the crust was completely covered by water. But land gradually emerged above the surface in three basic ways:

- Liquid rock welling up between separating plates hardened and piled up

- Masses of rock that became mountains were thrust up when two plates collided

- Lava from erupting volcanoes hardened into islands

As the Earth's plates drifted, several of these land masses began to merge to form the core of today's continents. About 5 percent of the current continental surface was formed by 3.5 billion years ago, about half by 2.5 billion years ago, and almost all by 500 million years ago. Today, the continents include about 57.7 million square miles, which represents 29.3 percent of the Earth's surface area.

Today, the continents include about 57.7 million square miles, which repre-sents 29.3 per-cent of the Earth's surface area.

DO WE KNOW WHAT THE WEATHER WAS LIKE BIL-LIONS OF YEARS AGO?

Hard as it is to believe, nearly all of the weather in the Earth's history has had the nerve to take place without weathermen to forecast it or weather instruments to record it. So, in peering back through time, we have to rely on subtle evidence carved into rocks, buried in the sediment on the ocean floor, or locked in fossilized remains of living things. Because the greatest proliferation of life didn't begin until 700 to 550 million years ago and because life on land didn't evolve until about 400 million years ago, it is particu-larly difficult to put an accurate, detailed chronology on the global climate in the seven-eighths of Earth's history. However, existing evidence does provide some fascinating glimpses into major events in the weather of long ago.

THE OCEANS FORM: 4.5 BILLION TO 4.2 BILLION YEARS AGO

And if you think your last vacation was ruined by weather, think about 300 million years of steady rain that fell from the young Earth's moisture-laden atmosphere. Gradually, this rain formed the oceans that covered the entire planet. Anyone cruising that worldwide ocean would had to have been patient for good weather—it wasn't until about 4.2 billion years ago, 355 million years after the Earth's birth, that the clouds cleared enough to provide the surface with its very first sunrise and sunset.

SUDDEN, VIOLENT UPHEAVAL: 4.2 BILLION TO 2.5 BILLION YEARS AGO

Because the moon was much closer, the Earth rotated about twice as fast as it does today. Powerful tides, gale winds, and strong ocean currents quickly reshaped and eroded emerging land masses that weren't protected by any vegetation. Prior to about 3.2 billion years ago, huge asteroids periodically slammed into the Earth, vaporizing the world's oceans. Scientists have discovered fossils of ancient, strange life forms, the evolution of which was abruptly ended by these catastrophes. Over the course of a few million years, rains would re-form the oceans, and evolution would begin again.

Finally, about 3 billion years ago, the climate stabilized somewhat, and life progressed to the point where vast blankets of algae covered much of the world's oceans.

THE FIRST GREAT ICE AGE: 2.5 BILLION TO 2 BILLION YEARS AGO

Scientists speculate that algae consumed so much of the carbon dioxide in the atmosphere that the greenhouse effect was greatly diminished and the Earth's temperature cooled. Glaciers formed, and by 2.3 billion years ago they covered most of the existing continental land masses. Fortunately for us, the amount of energy produced by the sun eventually reached its present levels. Over hundreds of millions of years, the glaciers melted.

A BILLION-YEAR WARM SPELL: 2 BILLION TO 950 MILLION YEARS AGO

We have very little detailed information about the climate in this long period. We do know that the continents became joined together in one long land mass about 1.5 billion years ago. The land that was the core of our present continent straddled the North Pole. However, it appears that global temperatures were significantly warmer than they are today, so North America was not covered by a permanent ice cap.

THE LONGEST WINTER: 950 TO 650 MILLION YEARS AGO

A second great ice age occurred between 950 million and 650 million years ago, a period called "the longest winter." No definitive explanation for this long period of global cooling has been

Scientists have discovered fossils of ancient, strange life forms, the evolution of which was abruptly ended by these catastrophes.

developed. The current belief is that a combination of factors were involved, including slight variations in the Earth's orbit around the sun, changes in ocean currents resulting from continental drift, changes in climate caused by continental uplift, and changes in the carbon dioxide content of the atmosphere.

During this time, the landmasses that are now Africa, South America, India, Madagascar, and Antarctica were joining in a supercontinent called Gondwanaland, which eventually drifted southward to the South Pole. That's why massive glacial deposits are found today in the Sahara Desert and the tropical regions of both Africa and South America.

THE GREAT WARMING: 650 MILLION YEARS AGO TO 70 MILLION YEARS AGO

As the Earth began to warm about 700 million years ago, a great proliferation of life began. By 550 million years ago, shell-fish had developed, leaving copious fossil records. Fish, including 30-foot-long carnivorous sharks, evolved by 450 million years ago. Shortly afterward, the first creatures crawled out onto land, and by 360 million years ago land life was proliferating.

During this entire time, temperatures were generally warm and the climate mild all over the globe. Water temperatures in high latitudes, 50 degrees to 60 degrees north, were an estimated 10 degrees higher than they are today.

This warming and the movement of continents explains geologic evidence found in the United States. From about 600 million to 400 million years ago, North America, Europe, Greenland, and parts of Asia were fused into a supercontinent called Laurasia, which lay along the equator. That's why we find in the United States today such relics of desert or tropical conditions as coral reefs, salt deposits left by evaporation, and red desert strata.

About 400 million years ago, Gondwanaland drifted back toward the equator and the huge ice cap covering it began to melt. Sea levels rose, flooding low-lying land all over the globe. This flooding covered the western United States with a vast sea, which left the fossil seashells we find today. Swamps and marshes covered Pennsylvania and other eastern states, and the remains of the dense vegetation were compressed into the vast seams of coal now being mined. Vegetation in seas covering what is now the Middle East decayed, producing most of the world's supply of oil.

As the continents flooded, they also moved back together. Around 300 million years ago, Gondwanaland and Laurasia collided to form a single continent called Pangaea, which was surrounded by the Panthalassa Ocean. By this time, dinosaurs had evolved and were beginning to flourish. With no oceans to bar migration, these giant reptiles and all other life forms spread through all the lands. That's why fossils of dinosaurs are found on every continent today.

70 MILLION YEARS AGO: EARTH COOLS OFF

The most recent ice ages, which produce our mental pictures of fur-clad cave men hunting mammoths, began with a gradual decline in the average temperature of Earth about 70 million years ago. Glaciers ebbed and flowed in cycles a few hundred thousand years apart, with the last ice age peaking about 18,000 years ago. At their peak, glaciers covered about one-third of Europe and about one-quarter of North America.

In the United States, the periods of glaciation are named for the states that now exist at the glaciers' farthest southern penetration. From earliest to latest, these periods are the Nebraskan age, the Kansan, the Illinoisan, and the Wisconsin.

As with "the longest winter," no comprehensive reason for these periods of global cooling has been developed. That's why long-term predictions about global weather trends are so difficult. Climatologists don't know whether we are experiencing a warmer lull between ice ages or whether we're about to enter a warmer period more typical of the Earth's climate over the last half billion years.

These long-term trends, however, have little to do with the dangers presented by global warming. The climate changes we've discussed in this chapter have taken place over tens, if not hundreds, of millions of years, a time frame allowing the environment ample time to adjust. A dramatic rise in global temperatures taking place over a matter of decades could be an environmental catastrophe.

THE EARTH'S ENVIRONMENTAL CATASTROPHES:
THE GREAT DYINGS

In the Earth's fossil records exists abundant evidence of, but not an explanation for, two massive environmental catastrophes that had profound effects on life on Earth. In the first, which occurred about a quarter billion years ago, life on Earth was almost completely wiped out in a very short period. More than 90 percent of all species became extinct. Of 50 families of mammal-like reptiles, 49 became extinct. Only one family survived to become the ancestors of man.

The difficulties of dating fossils from so long ago make it impossible to determine whether these extinctions took place over a few million years or in a much shorter time frame. That's why scientists have been unable to determine why the "Great Dying" occurred. Among the reasons put forth are the appearance of some natural chemical poison in the environment, the irradiation of Earth by the explosion of a nearby supernova, or the impact of an asteroid or comet.

However, strong evidence indicates that the impact of a massive asteroid wiped out all of the Earth's dinosaurs about 65 million years ago. This asteroid, an estimated six miles in diameter, may have crashed into the shallow ocean waters off Mexico's Yucatan Peninsula, creating a crater 120 miles in diameter. Within an hour, the massive debris thrown into space by the impact crashed back into the Earth's atmosphere. Red-hot from friction with the atmosphere, this debris ignited fires that burned almost all of the world's forests. Dust and smoke from these fires made it too dark to see on the Earth's surface for one to two months. For another two or three months, it was dark as full moonlight, and for a year it was too dark for plants to perform photosynthesis. At the same time, energy from the impact may have turned large amounts of nitrogen in the air into nitrous oxides, producing acid rain much more concentrated than that which falls today. As a result, smaller animals could manage to survive, but the dinosaurs that depended on massive quantities of plants for food became extinct.

That opened the door for the proliferation of mammals that eventually led to the evolution of both man and weatherman. At the end of this book, after I've explained what we've learned about the weather since that evolution, I'll take some time to peer into a crystal ball and explore the likelihood of further environmental catastrophes, both natural and man-made.

THE WEATHER'S ENGINE: OUR SUN

The sun is the source of almost all the energy that has, is, and ever will be used on Earth; the total energy that comes from starlight, moonlight, tidal forces, and the Earth's radioactivity totals just .02 percent of that provided by the star at the center of our solar system. Because our world is solar powered, the sun is the engine of the global weather machine.

HOW DOES THE SUN GENERATE ENERGY?

Our sun, like all other stars, is really a giant nuclear reactor in the sky. The first stars were formed about 14 billion years ago, about a billion years after the universe began with the "big bang," an explosion of a single point of infinite density and infinite temperature. Some of the tiny particles shot forth from this explosion eventually combined to form hydrogen and helium atoms. Random dispersion caused concentrations of these atoms, which were formed into clusters by the force of gravity. Gradually, gravity drew more and more atoms into balls that became increasingly hot as they became more dense and the atoms collided more frequently. When the temperatures reached about 20 million degrees, nuclear fusion began, a process that converted hydrogen atoms into helium atoms. The pressure from this conversion balanced the force of gravity, stabilizing these balls of atoms, which were now transformed into stars.

About 4.55 billion years ago, the explosion of a giant star somewhere in the universe disrupted a huge cloud of dust and gas in a part of the universe we call the Milky Way. The huge cloud broke up into a number of smaller clouds that condensed into stars. Some were twin stars that orbited each other, and a few consisted of groups of three or more stars. And one was a single star we call the sun.

About 4.55 billion years ago, the explosion of a giant star somewhere in the universe disrupted a huge cloud of dust and gas in a part of the universe we call the Milky Way.

THE SUN'S VITAL STATISTICS

Compared to the hundreds of billions of stars in the universe, our sun is slightly below average in size. Its diameter is 865,400 miles, its surface area is approximately 12,000 times that of Earth, and its mass is about 330,000 times that of our planet.

The average distance of the sun from the Earth is about 93 million miles, which is used as a unit of measurement called an Astronomical Unit (A.U.). The Earth is closest to the sun in January (91.5 million miles) and farthest away in July (94.5 million miles), but these variations don't have a measurable effect on our weather. The light from the sun takes approximately 8.5 minutes to reach Earth (the speed of light is 186,000 miles per second), so that distance can also be expressed as 8.5 light-minutes. By comparison, the nearest star, Alpha Centauri, is about 4.3 light-years away.

While Earth revolves around the sun, the sun revolves around the center of the Milky Way at a speed of about 175 miles per second. One revolution—a solar year—takes about 220 million Earth years. Meanwhile, the whole galaxy is moving through space toward the constellation Hercules at about 12 miles per second.

THE SUN'S ENERGY OUTPUT

It took more than 2 billion years for the sun's "furnace" to reach full efficiency; initially the sun gave off less than 75 percent of the energy that it does today. Now, with the furnace fully stoked, the sun's internal temperature is an estimated 36 million degrees Fahrenheit and the surface temperature is about 11,000 degrees. The sun burns 4 million tons of hydrogen every second, producing this awesome amount of energy:

- An area of the sun's surface the size of a postage stamp gives off enough energy to power 500 60-watt light bulbs.

- One horsepower is the amount of energy necessary to lift 33,000 pounds a distance of 1 foot for 1 minute. Each square yard of the sun emits 72,000 horsepower. The sun's average total output in horsepower is 500 followed by 21 zeros.

Because the sun radiates energy 360 degrees, Earth intercepts only a tiny portion—just one part in two billion. Yet that seemingly insignificant percentage amounts to 5 million horsepower per square mile of Earth's surface. If the amount of the sun's energy that hits the Earth in one hour could be trapped and harnessed, it would meet the world's total annual energy needs. To replace the energy received from the sun in just one day we would have to burn 700 billion tons of coal.

The amount of solar energy that reaches the Earth is just the right amount to sustain life. If the amount of sunlight were cut by just 10 percent, our planet would be a frozen ball of ice.

While Earth revolves around the sun, the sun revolves around the center of the Milky Way at a speed of about 175 miles per second.

COULD YOU STAND ON THE SURFACE OF THE SUN?

Because the sun is a ball of gases, it doesn't have a firm surface like that of Earth, the moon, and the other inner planets. The intense gravity of the sun means, however, that much of the gas has a density thousands of times that of the densest metal on Earth. But even assuming it were possible to construct a space-suit insulated enough to withstand the heat, it would be impossible to make that suit strong enough to withstand the air pressure of the sun, which is 200 billion times that of Earth.

DOES THE SUN HAVE WEATHER?

Although the sun appears to us like a smooth giant light bulb in the sky, it has its own forms of violent weather. The most visible evidence of solar storms is sunspots, areas of the sun that appear darker because they are cooler (about 7,500 degrees Fahrenheit) than the rest of the surface. A sunspot is really a hurricane of whirling gases generated by powerful magnetic fields inside the sun. These storms, which range from 500 to 50,000 miles in diameter, rise to the surface about 30 or 40 degrees north or south of the sun's equator. They rage for a few days to a week until they die out as they approach the equator. Associated with sunspots are solar prominences or flares, fiery eruptions that send spikes of hot gas as far as 250,000 miles into space. Although sunspots are cooler than the rest of the sun's surface, their appearance coincides with an increase in the sun's energy output of about .2 percent.

One of the great mysteries about the sun is why the number of sunspots normally peak in a cycle that usually lasts eleven years, but can range from seven to 17 years. During the down year of a cycle, as few as a dozen sunspots may appear. During the peak year, thousands may occur.

Sunspots have been noticed since the 13th or 14th century. In 1611, Galileo studied sunspots and used them to calculate the speed of the sun's rotation. In the mid-19th century, a British astronomer named E. Walter Maunder discovered volumes of records of sunspot sightings dating back more than 200 years. These records showed that sunspots disappeared entirely between 1645 and 1715, a period of 70 years.

HOW DOES THE SUN'S ENERGY GET TO EARTH?

The sun emits an enormous range of energy, of which the light we're so familiar with is only a part. The sun puts forth huge volumes of ultra-violet rays, infrared rays, x-rays, microwaves, radio waves, as well as an assortment of charged particles. All these different kinds of energy are forms of electromagnetic radiation that travels through the vacuum of space as waves. Unlike waves in the ocean that move the water they travel in, electromagnetic waves don't move air and don't require air to move.

However, when they encounter something, they give up some or all of their energy. As I'll discuss shortly, our atmosphere serves as a shield against the most harmful types of this energy. The visible light and some infrared energy that get through provide the heat that warms our planet.

How the remaining energy is absorbed by our planet depends on what it encounters. The amount of energy reflected back into space varies as follows:

Feature	Percentange of sun's energy reflected back into the air
Fresh snow	75% to 90%
Thick clouds	75% to 90%
Thin clouds	30% to 50%
Sand	15% to 45%
Grassy field	10% to 30%
Water	10%
Forests	3% to 10%

Unlike waves in the ocean that move the water they travel in, electromagnetic waves don't move air and don't require air to move.

From this table, it's easy to understand why the polar regions are so frigid. It also vividly demonstrates the importance of the oceans and the world's forests in trapping the energy that makes Earth warm enough to support life.

DOES THE SUN'S WEATHER AFFECT OUR WEATHER?

Radiation from intense solar storms bombards our upper atmosphere, which can play havoc with radio communications. But despite massive research efforts, no one has been able to prove that the sunspot cycle has any specific direct effects on the world's day-to-day weather. Meteorologists now suspect that if any short-term effects do exist, they are minor.

However, solar astronomers have compiled compelling evidence linking the absence of sunspots between 1645 and 1715 with the Little Ice Age, a prolonged spell of cold weather that affected northern Europe at the same time.

IF THE SUN'S ENERGY REMAINS CONSTANT, WHY DO WE HAVE SEASONS?

The sun's energy output doesn't remain exactly constant—in

fact, there are slight long-term variations that may combine with variations in the Earth's orbit that influence weather over the course of tens of thousands of years. But short-term changes, such as the change in seasons, don't result from changes in the sun. Rather, we have seasons because the Earth is tilted on its axis about 23.5 degrees, an angle that doesn't change. That means that as the Earth revolves around the sun, the northern hemisphere is tilted toward the sun for half the year, while the southern hemisphere is tilted toward the sun for the other half of the year.

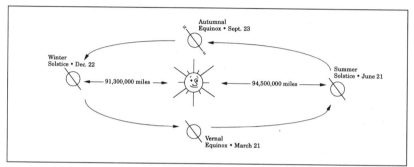

The Earth's tilt is a blessing, because the change in seasons helps distribute heat more widely around the globe.

The more directly the sun shines on a part of the Earth, the more energy that part receives. To understand why, find a flashlight and sit at a table in a darkened room. If you hold the flashlight over the table and point it straight down, a strong beam of concentrated light appears on the table. As you tilt the flashlight at an angle, the beam spreads out and the light becomes noticeably weaker.

The Earth's tilt is a blessing, because the change in seasons helps distribute heat more widely around the globe. If the Earth didn't tilt, the area of the Earth around the equator would be unbearably hot year-round, while the northern and southern regions would be permanently frozen.

THE SEASONS WHERE WE ARE

Twice a year, on or about March 21 and September 21, the sun is directly overhead at the equator. The hours of daylight and the hours of darkness are about equal all over the globe, so in the northern hemisphere we call these dates the vernal (Spring) equinox and the autumnal (Fall) equinox.

After March 21, the point at which the sun shines directly overhead moves slowly northward. On or about June 21, the summer solstice, the sun is directly overhead at its northernmost point, a line around the globe that runs through central Mexico, brushes northern Cuba, bisects the Sahara Desert and the Arabian Peninsula, then runs through northern India, southern China, and the Hawaiian Islands. This line is called the Tropic of Cancer. On the summer solstice, the northern hemisphere enjoys its longest hours of daylight. Because the North Pole is tilted most directly at the sun, polar regions experience 24-hour days.

In contrast, the point at which the sun shines directly overhead moves slowly southward after September 21. On or about December 21, the winter solstice, the sun is overhead at its southernmost point (the Tropic of Capricorn), while it is at its lowest point in the sky in the northern hemisphere. On the winter solstice, we endure our longest night, and in the region of the North Pole, darkness remains 24 hours per day. The line around the globe at the northernmost point that has at least some daylight every day of the year is called the Arctic Circle. (The complementary line around the southern polar regions is called the Antarctic Circle.)

WHAT IS THE FUTURE OF THE SUN?

You shouldn't put the sun burning out at the top of your worry list, because solar astronomers estimate it has enough hydrogen to last another 5 billion years. As this fuel runs out, the sun will begin to turn red as it increases dramatically in size, becoming what astronomers call a red giant. The expanding sun will certainly engulf Mercury, and possibly even Venus and Earth. Even if it doesn't expand this far, everything on this planet will be burned to a crisp. Then, when the nuclear reactor is extinguished, gravity will cause the sun to suddenly collapse into a white dwarf, a dense Earth-size object. The Earth will become a frigid, barren, airless ball of rock.

On the winter solstice, we endure our longest night, and in the region of the North Pole, darkness remains 24 hours per day.

THE ATMOSPHERE: THE OCEAN OF AIR IN WHICH WE LIVE

I f you were ever a Superman fan, as I was, you probably spent a little time thinking about how remarkable his skin was. Somehow, it was soft, warm, but at the same time, it provided perfect protection from bullets, knives, arrows, blunt instruments, and all other kinds of bad stuff. Skin like that was just too miraculous to be true.

At least, that's what I thought before I became a weatherman. Then I realized: the atmosphere, the "skin" of our planet, performs the same miracle as Superman's skin. It lets through the visible light and heat that provide almost all of our planet's energy, while providing nearly perfect protection from solar radiation, x-rays, ultraviolet rays, meteors, and other bad stuff that make the rest of our solar system so hostile to unprotected life. This shield of air, which took billions of years to form, became the ultimate in cosmic armor.

Of course, the atmosphere is a thin "skin" only when viewed in proportion to the Earth it covers; to us, it is a vast ocean of air that swirls around and above us. We tend to think of the atmosphere as extending upward only to the tops of the clouds, because this layer alone contains the weather that occupies so much of our interest. Only recently, when the phrase "ozone layer" has begun to reach the headlines, have we begun to realize that the atmosphere is a sophisticated structure composed of complex layers that nurture and sustain life.

3

Nature experimented for 4 billion years before the recipe for air was right for life.

HOW DID WE FIND OUT WHAT AIR WAS MADE OF?

As we discussed earlier, Nature experimented for 4 billion years before the recipe for air was right for life. Remember, the first atmosphere was the combustible mixture of hydrogen and helium, which gave way to a thick stew of carbon dioxide and water vapor before algae went to work and turned it into the third-generation atmosphere we have today. But even though we human beings developed as a result of this new air, a very large percentage of our time on Earth passed before we figured out the recipe. Long ago, in the fifth century B.C., a Greek philosopher named Empedocles postulated that air was an unfathomable substance that was one of the four basic elements (the others being earth, water, and fire) from which everything is derived. Approximately a century later, Aristotle took Empedocles's theory and expanded upon it, saying each of the four elements had its place in the natural order. Earth was on the bottom, with water, air, and fire above. That's why anything made of earth, such as a rock, fell. Water fell as rain, too, because its place was below air. Fire, on the other hand, always rose.

For nearly 1,800 years, any questioning of Aristotle's philosophy was squelched by the intellectual establishment. Then, with the dawning of the Renaissance, the best minds began substituting scientific experimentation for philosophy. In order for us to understand the properties of the air around us, it helps to explore the difficult but exciting detective stories that led to the first discoveries of these properties.

MYSTERY NUMBER 1: DOES AIR HAVE WEIGHT?

Our first great detective was an Italian astronomer and physicist named Galileo Galilei. Among his many brilliant discoveries was the fact that objects fall at the same speed regardless of their weight, which he and others proved by dropping rocks of different weights from the top of tall buildings and observing them hit the ground at the same time. However, a feather took a lot longer to float down than a rock. Galileo believed that the problem wasn't his theory, but the fact that air was a measurable substance that offered resistance.

So he devised another experiment. He fitted a large, narrow-necked glass flask with a rubber stopper, then injected large quantities of air with a syringe. When he weighed the flask afterward, it was heavier. He concluded that air does have weight and calculated that weight as 460 times lighter than water—impressively close to the real figure of 810 times lighter than water, considering Galileo's crude instruments.

MYSTERY NUMBER 2: HOW CAN THAT WEIGHT BE MEASURED?

Galileo died before he could explore other mysteries about air. But his assistant, Evangelista Torricelli, was especially intrigued by this one mystery: No matter how strong a suction pump was used, well water could not be raised in a pipe higher than 34 feet. Other scientists, who believed that water was drawn up the suction pipe when a vacuum was created, postulated that there was a limit to the so-called pulling power of a vacuum. Torricelli wasn't sure, and he decided to investigate.

The major problem was that devising an experiment with a 34-foot-long pipe full of water was very awkward. The answer was using a liquid heavier than water so a shorter tube could be used. Torricelli settled on mercury, which is 14 times heavier than water.

The experiment he devised was as follows: He filled a glass tube three feet long with mercury, then plugged the open end with his finger. He turned the tube upside down and submerged it in a basin of mercury. The level of mercury in the tube fell until it settled at a level of about 30 inches. Torricelli experimented with several tubes of different sizes, but no matter what the size, the level of the mercury was the same height. His conclusion: The height of the mercury in the tube was determined by the pressure of the air on the mercury in the basin, not on any pulling force of the vacuum created on the other end of the tube. He had invented a barometer, a device for measuring air pressure. Today we still measure air pressure in inches of mercury.

MYSTERY NUMBER 3: WHAT CAUSES AIR PRESSURE?

Our next sleuth was the great French mathematician Blaise Pascal, who was intrigued by the invention of the barometer. Pascal decided that the pressure on the ground was created by the mass of air above. If that were true, then air pressure should drop as the elevation rises.

Pascal was very frail and was terrified of heights, so he enlisted his brother-in-law, a government official who lived in the French Alps, to carry out an experiment. With monks as reliable witnesses, the brother-in-law constructed a barometer at the base of a mountain which measured 28 inches of mercury. With a monk watching that barometer like a hawk, the rest of the party scaled a 4,888-foot peak and built another barometer. When the mercury rose to only 24.5 inches, a great cheer went up. Pascal was right—air pressure did result from the weight of the air piled up above.

MYSTERY NUMBER 4: WHAT IS AIR MADE OF?

The realization that air had weight that increased as more was "piled on" led to the idea that air was not one substance, but a mixture of different kinds of invisible particles. The search for those substances was carried on by several scientists over a period of 150 years.

First on board with a discovery was English scientist Robert Boyle. He and his assistant Robert Hooke placed mice, birds, and other creatures in glass jars and watched. Over a period of time, the animals would pant and weaken, but would revive if released. The same held true for combustion. A candle in a glass jar would eventually go out; it would also burn longer in compressed air. Boyle and Hooke concluded that there was some substance in air necessary for life—they called it "vital air." Much later it would be known as "oxygen."

Nothing was added to this concept for 100 years, until a Scottish medical student named Joseph Black discovered that limestone treated with acid gave off a strange kind of air that extinguished flames and killed small animals. Because this kind of air could be trapped by use of lime or magnesium, Black called it "fixed air." He found that "fixed air" was especially prevalent in exhaled human breath and in the bubbles given off by fermenting beer. We now refer to "fixed air" as carbon dioxide.

About 20 years later, a student of Black named Daniel Rutherford decided to find out what was left after "fixed air" and "vital air" were removed from air. After several false starts, he found a way to absorb both the carbon dioxide and the oxygen in liquid. The air that was left, which made up about three-quarters of the original volume, instantly extinguished both flames and life. Rutherford called it "noxious air"; we call it nitrogen.

AIR: OUR MODERN, SOPHISTICATED VIEW

Sophisticated modern instruments confirm the brilliant deductions of our great scientific detectives: Air is a mixture of gases, along with some foreign particles. Its primary components are nitrogen (78 percent) and oxygen (21 percent), and this ratio is consistent all over our planet. Carbon dioxide makes up just .034 percent of our air, but that small level is crucial to the balance of life on Earth. Other gases such as ozone, carbon monoxide, sulfur dioxide, and methane also play a role in sustaining life. At any given time, air contains water vapor that varies from almost none in desert areas to 4 percent of the volume of air in tropical rain forests. Finally, air holds varying amounts of solid particles, such as dust, salt, pollen, chemicals, and material from volcanic eruptions or meteors.

WHAT WE NOW KNOW ABOUT AIR PRESSURE

All those little molecules in air zip around at great speeds—an average of a little over 1,000 miles an hour. Although air is only about 1/800 as dense as water, it is still packed tightly enough that one molecule only has to move 1-millionth of an inch before it collides with another molecule. The collective movement of these molecules creates air pressure pushing out in all directions—imagine millions of little people crowded inside a balloon trying to push their way out.

About 5.75 quadrillion tons of air blanket the Earth's 197 million square miles of surface, or about .08 pound per cubic foot. The average air pressure at sea level is 14.7 pounds per square inch, or about a ton of pressure on the average-size person. We don't feel it, however—the air inside our bodies balances with the air outside.

The specific air pressure changes constantly. We weatherpeople usually give the pressure in inches of mercury, and the average worldwide air pressure is 29.9212 inches. However, cold air produces higher air pressure than warm air. A drop in air pressure of just 1 inch of mercury can produce a major storm, while a rise of 1 inch will mean delightful fair weather.

A drop in air pressure of just 1 inch of mercury can produce a major storm, while a rise of 1 inch will mean delightful fair weather.

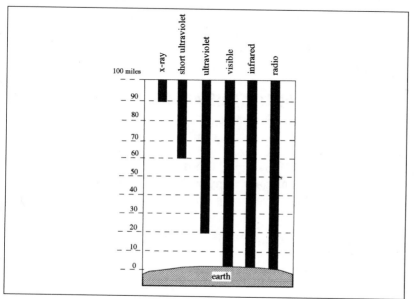

How the Earth's atmosphere repels harmful rays.

Air pressure changes at ground level take place so gradually that our bodies can't detect them. However, some other creatures are more sensitive, and their behaviors can be predictors of approaching storms.

WHY DO OUR EARS POP IN AN ELEVATOR OR AN AIRPLANE?

Air pressure drops about .1 inch of mercury for every 100 feet in elevation. When our elevation increases rapidly, in an airplane taking off or in an elevator, the outside pressure drops more quickly than our inside pressure, producing discomfort in our ears. The "pop" we feel is air escaping through our eustachian tubes to even the pressure. If our eustachian tube is blocked, perhaps as a result of a cold, the pressure of air pushing outward against the eardrum can produce excruciating pain. The best way to relieve the pressure is to yawn, chew gum, or hold your nose and blow with your mouth closed.

When we descend, the situation is reversed. The outside air pressure rises more quickly and pushes inward against our eardrums, causing pain until the pressure equalizes.

HOW RAPIDLY DOES AIR PRESSURE DECREASE WITH HEIGHT?

Half of all our air (in volume) is below 18,000 feet, the point at which the air pressure is only 7.5 pounds per square inch. The air pressure drops in half again, to about 3.75 pounds per square inch, at 36,000 feet. At 100,000 feet, 99 percent of all air is below.

The decrease in air pressure caused by a decrease in the volume of the air is what makes it so difficult to breathe at high altitudes.

HOW IS ALL THIS AIR ARRANGED?

To continue our earlier analogy, the air in our atmosphere forms layers with different functions, just like the layers of our skin. Although some of these layers are far above us, damage to one of them, such as the ozone layer, could cause serious damage to life on Earth, just as damage to a layer of skin can cause infection.

The all-important layers of our atmosphere are:

• The *troposphere* extends from ground level to a height of 6 to 11 miles, depending on latitude and the season of the year. The greenhouse effect keeps the temperatures warm near the surface, but the temperature drops steadily as the altitude increases. The top of the troposphere is the point at which temperatures stop becoming cooler.

This temperature change is why the troposphere contains almost all of our weather. The warm, moisture-laden air that forms clouds continues to rise as long as the air above is cooler. But when the temperature stops dropping, upward movement stops and so do the clouds. That's why the tops of thunderclouds spread out in a flat, anvil shape as they reach the "ceiling" of the troposphere.

• The *stratosphere* extends from the troposphere to about 30 miles above the surface. The mixture of nitrogen (78 percent), oxygen (21 percent), and carbon dioxide (.003 percent) is about the same as the lower level. But this level also contains the ozone layer, which is strongest between 12 and 24 miles high.

Molecules of ozone absorb the sun's ultraviolet rays, providing crucial protection for life on Earth. Some infrared rays are also absorbed in the stratosphere. Because it absorbs energy, the stratosphere is warmer than the troposphere, having a temperature of about 32 degrees Fahrenheit at an altitude of 30 miles.

• The *mesosphere* ranges from 30 to 50 miles above the surface. No heat is absorbed in this layer, and the temperature plunges to minus 148 degrees Fahrenheit at its outer limits.

• The *thermosphere*, or *ionosphere*, extends from 50 to 250 miles. The air consists mostly of nitrogen molecules to 125 miles and mostly oxygen molecules above that. The crucial role of this layer is to filter out the x-rays and gamma rays from the sun. These rays are absorbed by atoms of nitrogen or oxygen, each of which gives off one electron, which becomes a positively charged ion. These ions reflect radio waves, and are used to bounce back radio waves transmitted from the surface.

• The *exosphere* extends from 250 to about 435 miles, at which point space begins. This level has few atoms and is mostly a vacuum.

• The *magnetosphere* includes the exosphere but extends beyond to a distance of 40,000 to 80,000 miles. It represents the Earth's external magnetic field. At altitudes of 1,850 miles and 9,300 miles are regions of filled with particles trapped by this magnetic field, regions known as the Van Allen belts. Particles spilling out of these belts spiral toward the Earth's poles, producing the spectacles of the northern and southern lights.

This multi-layer sandwich of air above us makes life possible by trapping the sun's heat and filtering out dangerous parts of the energy coming from the sun. Only visible light, some infrared light, and radio waves reach the surface. The atmosphere also intercepts vast majority of meteorites entering Earth's orbit.

WHAT IS THE SKY?

The word *sky* has two different meanings, depending on whether you're an astronomer or a meteorologist. To an astronomer, looking to the skies means scanning the entire expanse of the universe. This sky has an expanse of billions of light-years, far beyond our sight and comprehension.

To us weatherpeople, *sky* means the part of the atmosphere that affects our climate here on Earth. When we watch the skies, we're looking for clouds, wind direction, precipitation, and anything else that influences weather. From a weather standpoint, "as high as the sky" means at the upper limit of the troposphere, somewhere between 5 and 12 miles above us.

WHY IS THE SKY BLUE?

In the outer reaches of our atmosphere, the sky is black. But as light passes through the stratosphere, it begins to encounter air molecules. These molecules scatter the blue and violet wavelengths, but allow the rest of the light to pass through untouched. This scattered blue and violet light makes the sky look blue.

WATER: THE WELLSPRING OF LIFE

If an observer from another galaxy were to drop into our solar system and catalog its celestial bodies, no doubt Earth would be described as the "water planet." Almost three-quarters of the planet's surface (71 percent), is covered in water that gives Earth its distinctive blue appearance from space. Early in its existence, our world was completely covered by one immense ocean, and in these waters life was miraculously created. Although we take the oceans for granted, they play a crucial role in maintaining a climate and environment that allow the continued existence of life.

Even though the total volume of Earth's water is 326 million cubic miles, 97 percent of that is in the oceans.

All of us more easily understand that life on Earth couldn't exist without fresh water. But because we're so used to water gushing out at the turn of a tap, we don't fully understand how precarious a resource it is. Even though the total volume of Earth's water is 326 million cubic miles (at more than 26 billion gallons per cubic mile, an incomprehensible amount), 97 percent of that is in the oceans. Another 2.1 percent is locked up the ice caps, leaving less than 1 percent for all the people, animals, and plants in the world. To put it further in perspective, if all the water on Earth were represented by 25 gallons, all life would have to exist on just one teaspoon.

That teaspoonful of water is constantly being recycled through the atmosphere. It forms clouds and condenses into the rain, snow, sleet, and hail that provide so much of our weather.

WHERE DID OUR WATER COME FROM?

Because of the intense direct bombardment of the sun, when the young Earth was three-quarters its present size, it had less water than the next outer planet, Mars. However, the intense heat in the Earth's core released water trapped in rocks as they melted, and formed more by combining two hydrogen atoms with one atom of oxygen. After the magma seas hardened into a crust, numerous volcanoes spewed forth gases that consisted of carbon dioxide and 60 percent to 70 percent water vapor. Because the sun at that time shone with only 75 percent of its current intensity, the average temperature of the Earth was only about 52 degrees Fahrenheit. In these cool temperatures, this water vapor condensed easily and fell as rain, forming the first lakes and oceans. The clouds generated by volcanoes were so thick that it may have taken 200 million years of torrential rains to condense enough moisture out of the sky to allow the sun to shine through. At the same time, ice-rich planetesimals thrown toward the sun by the formation of the huge outer planets frequently struck Earth and melted, adding to the water supply. By that time, about 4.2 billion years ago, the fully formed Earth was completely covered by one gigantic ocean.

A t any given time, there's only enough water in the atmosphere to drop one inch of rain over all the Earth's surface, just a 10-to-12-day supply.

WHERE IS OUR WATER TODAY?

The amount of water in our biosphere (another name for our environment) has neither increased nor decreased in billions of years. Today, the vast majority of all water, 97.2 percent, is salt water in the oceans. The distribution of our freshwater is:

	Volume (cubic miles)	Percent of total
All freshwater lakes	30,000	0.009
All rivers	300	.0001
Antarctic ice cap	6,300,000	1.9
Arctic ice cap & glaciers	680,000	0.21
Water in atmosphere	3,100	0.001
Ground water within 1/2 mile of surface	1,000,000	0.31
Deep ground water	1,000,000	0.31
Total fresh water	10,013,400	2.7391

Fresh water in lakes and rivers would soon disappear if it weren't replenished by rain or snow. At any given time, there's only enough water in the atmosphere to drop one inch of rain over all the Earth's surface, just a 10- to-12-day supply. Fortunately, an immense amount of water is constantly evaporating from the oceans—104 million billion gallons, about one quarter of the oceans' total volume, evaporates every year. Most of this water falls back in the ocean. But some is blown over land, falling as rain or snow to replenish freshwater supplies. It replaces water that makes its way down streams or rivers into the ocean.

HOW DOES WATER DISAPPEAR INTO THE AIR?

The idea that something tangible like water could "disappear" into the air, then reappear as rain seemed so magical to the

I don't generally do the flying myself, but aerial weather monitoring plays a crucial role in modern forecasting.

ancients that they conjured up rain gods who produced precipitation by opening some invisible celestial stream or by some other supernatural process. By the 17th century, the best explanation scientists could come up with was that liquid water somehow formed tiny hollow drops filled with the air that floated upward like soap bubbles until they "popped" and fell as rain. But about the time our friends Boyle and Hooke discovered that air was a mixture of gases, another English chemist named John Dalton arrived at the correct conclusion that water vapor was in fact a gas that mixed with the other gases in the air.

This discovery made apparent the fact that water is the Houdini of substances, because it has the altogether magical ability to exist in solid, liquid, and gaseous states at the same time. These states are determined by the behavior of individual water molecules.

- Ice: At colder temperatures, water molecules are locked together in crystals, vibrating but not moving.

- Liquid water: As temperatures warm, these molecules gain enough energy to begin to break free and move around, but not enough to break away from each other. Because there is more space between molecules locked into crystals than between the molecules milling around in the liquid, ice is less dense than water.

- Water vapor: When molecules gain enough energy to attain the speed necessary to break free of other molecules, they escape to mix with the other gases that make up air. Since this

By the 17th century, scientists believed that water somehow formed tiny hollow drops filled with the air that floated upward like soap bubbles until they "popped" and fell as rain.

escape requires absorbing heat energy, the surface the molecules leave behind is cooler. That's why evaporating perspiration cools our skin.

WANT A QUESTION THAT'S SURE TO STUMP YOUR FRIENDS?

That question is: What's heavier, dry air or damp air? We think of water as heavier than air, so odds are your friends will say damp air. But believe it or not, a molecule of water vapor is lighter than a molecule of oxygen or nitrogen. Every molecule of water vapor that enters a volume of air kicks out an oxygen or nitrogen molecule. The result: The more water vapor, the lighter the air.

HOW MUCH WATER VAPOR CAN AIR HOLD?

Every time you see water form on the outside of a glass filled with ice you're roughly duplicating the scientific experiment that unlocked the mystery of how water in the air affects the weather. The year was 1751 when a French physicist named Charles Le Roy sealed damp air in a glass container and watched. As the container cooled, drops of moisture formed on the sides. When Le Roy heated the container, the drops disappeared. From this and similar experiments, Le Roy formulated the following important principle:

- The amount of water vapor air can hold increases dramatically as the temperature increases.

Let's say a specific volume of air at 32 degrees Fahrenheit can hold a cup of water. That same volume of air can hold a pint of water at 50 degrees, a quart of water at 72 degrees, and more than half a gallon at 95 degrees. That's why we use heat to dry our hair and our clothes.

And what happens when the air is cooled? Its capacity shrinks, but the amount of water vapor stays the same. The effect is like pouring water from a half-gallon container into a quart container into a pint container into a cup container. No matter how much water you start with, one container is bound to overflow. After much experimentation, our friend Charles Le Roy stated the principle this way:

- Any specific volume of air has a specific temperature at which the water vapor it contains will begin to return to liquid form.

We call this temperature the dew point, after the dew on the grass that results when the air temperature drops on a clear night.

Any specific volume of air has a specific temperature at which the water vapor it contains will begin to return to liquid form.

At this temperature, the air is completely saturated, which means precipitation or fog is likely.

WHAT IS HUMIDITY AND WHAT DOES IT MEAN?

Humidity is the amount of water vapor in the air, a measurement that doesn't tell us much about how comfortable we are or what the weather is likely to be. For example, the air during a heavy winter snowstorm in the United States. contains less moisture than the cloudless skies over the Sahara Desert. The amount of water vapor in 60-degree air in San Francisco would bring a damp, bone-chilling fog and drizzle, but in 85-degree sunny Los Angeles, would contribute to a comfortable, brilliantly sunny beach day.

The reason is that the likelihood of precipitation and the degree to which the air feels damp or dry doesn't depend on the amount of water vapor in a specific volume, but rather the actual amount of water relative to the maximum amount of water the air could hold at that temperature.This ratio is called the relative humidity; when your local weatherperson says the humidity is 65 percent, he or she really means the relative humidity is 65 percent—in other words, the air holds about two-thirds of the water vapor it could potentially hold at that temperature. The relative humidity constantly changes with the temperature.

We see the importance of relative humidity every winter in the northern United States. Freezing air holds very little moisture. When that air enters our homes and is heated to 70 degrees, the relative humidity plunges to levels lower than the driest deserts. To return the humidity to comfortable levels, we purchase humidifiers to put water vapor into the air. In the summer, on the other hand, warm air descends to our basements, which tend to be cooler than the rest of the house. The result is dampness that can produce mildew, unless we run a dehumidifier to take water out of the air.

Relative humidity has other practical applications. For example, clothes can hang on a line all day without drying when the humidity is 85 percent or 90 percent. On the other hand, dehydration during exercise is a danger when the humidity is very low—perspiration evaporates so quickly that we feel cool until we run out of fluid and overheat.

Relative humidity helps us understand our external weather, too. For example, you can see why we get our heaviest rains when cold air runs into warm, damp air. On the other hand, the weather clears when warm air replaces cold, damp air. When the relative humidity is close to 100 percent during the day, we're likely to have fog at night when the air cools.

When the relative humidity is close to 100 percent during the day, we're likely to have fog at night when the air cools.

DOES THE RELATIVE HUMIDITY HAVE TO BE 100 PERCENT BEFORE PRECIPITATION FALLS?

Oh, would that predicting precipitation were so simple! Unfortunately, the combined effects of the sun, the atmosphere, and the amount of water vapor in different parcels of air lead to a variety of weather conditions. To understand exactly how water vapor is returned to us as precipitation, we first have to explore the fascinating story of clouds.

SKYWATCHING: EVERYTHING YOU WANT TO KNOW ABOUT CLOUDS

A t any given time, clouds cover about 60 percent of the Earth's skies. In ancient times, when sailors and farmers couldn't flip on the radio or television for a forecast, they studied the clouds for clues about changes in the weather. As early as 300 B.C., the Greek philosopher Theophrastus published his *Book of Signs*, which included 100 variations of clouds that foretold certain types of weather. Today, with all of our sophisticated instruments and banks of computers, studying the clouds is still a quick and effective way of predicting upcoming weather changes.

We've discovered that clouds hold just .001 percent of the world's water, yet the role they play in distributing that water to the ground below is vital to the entire water cycle. Clouds also moderate the Earth's climate. Clouds reflect part of the heat from the sun back into space, keeping parts of our planet from becoming too warm. The clouds also trap heat radiating from the ground, which keeps the Earth from becoming too cool.

Finally, clouds can be a source of awe-inspiring beauty, providing the canvas upon which sunset and sunrises are painted. The more we learn about the types of clouds, the more we appreciate the variety and beauty with which nature has chosen to adorn our planet.

In ancient times, sailors and farmers studied the clouds for clues about changes in the weather.

WHAT IS A CLOUD?

A cloud is a portion of air in which water vapor has condensed into visible moisture. Clouds result when air rises and is cooled to the dew point. Depending on the height above the ground, the moisture condenses as water droplets or freezes as ice crystals.

THE SURPRISING KEY TO CLOUD FORMATION: DIRTY AIR

We tend to think that air pollution is bad for our environment, and in fact, the existence of many chemicals in the atmosphere is harmful to life. But if the atmosphere were perfectly clean, there would be no clouds, no gentle rain, and maybe, no life on Earth.

The reason is a strange property of water vapor that scientists discovered when they sealed damp air in a tube and cooled it to the dew point. Moisture would form the first time or two, but then the air would remain clear, no matter how cold the air got. When fresh air was let into the tube, moisture formed again. This puzzle stumped researchers until a Frenchman named Paul Jean Coulier put forth a theory that water vapor tends to condense around tiny particles of dust, such as salt spray from the ocean, volcanic dust, particles resulting from combustion, dust from meteors, and almost everything else that breaks up into small parts.

It turns out that these particles, which are called "condensation nuclei," are incredibly small. More than 5,000 of the tiniest of these particles can be crammed into a cubic centimeter. The larger ones are as thick as the film on a soap bubble, while the giants are 1/10 as thick as a human hair.

Wind patterns that blow certain types of particles in certain directions are linked to weather patterns. For example, prevailing winds blow dust from North Africa across the Atlantic to South America, and expansion and contraction of the Sahara Desert has been linked to expansion and contraction of the rain forests.

Without these particles in the air, water would evaporate without forming clouds until the air was supersaturated. Periodically, this moisture would abruptly condense and fall as massive, incredibly destructive downpours that would cause ruinous erosion.

HOW DOES AIR RISE TO FORM CLOUDS?

There are three basic ways in which air rises to form clouds. The first occurs when a surface is warmed by the sun, which in turn warms the air above it. This air rises in a vertical column to form puffy fair weather clouds or, when the air is especially warm and damp, thunderclouds.

Clouds also form when two air masses collide. Since cold air is heavier than warm air, an approaching cold front wedges under the warm air, lifting it. An approaching warm front slides over a cold air mass, cooling air in the contact zone. Both types of collision form thick layers of clouds.

Finally, air is lifted by mountains or other large landmasses until it cools and forms clouds that often shroud the peaks.

WHY DON'T CLOUDS FALL FROM THE SKY?

For centuries, men of scientific bent spent untold hours trying to figure out why clouds seemed to be immune to the forces of gravity that pulled everything, including water drops, toward the Earth. Among the fanciful solutions offered to this puzzle was the theory that water in the air consisted of tiny bubbles floating upward like balloons. But it wasn't until this century that we finally learned that cloud droplets are incredibly small, less than 1/2500 of an inch in diameter. It takes more than 1 million cloud droplets to form an average raindrop. You'd need to collect as many as 7 billion droplets to make a tablespoon of water. Only trying to count the grains of sand on a beach is comparable to trying to calculate the incredible number of these droplets that form the average puffy cloud drifting overhead on a summer day.

Every object that falls from a high enough height, from a steel ball to a feather, has a terminal velocity, a point at which air pressure balances the additional pull of gravity. Because they are so small and light, cloud droplets have a terminal velocity, or maximum rate of fall, of .02 miles per hour, or about 2 feet per minute. The slightest updraft will stop their descent as the cloud blows along with the wind. Those that do drift into warmer air evaporate quickly.

WHY ARE CLOUDS WHITE?

If you stop to think about it, it might seem that clouds made up of water droplets should be clear, like a cup of water. But that's not the case. You may remember from our description of the atmosphere that the sky is blue because air molecules scatter blue and violet light wavelengths and let the others through. Cloud droplets are much bigger than air molecules, so they scatter and mix all the colors, making the sunlight that passes through them look white. However, if the clouds are especially thick, not all the light makes it through, which is why some clouds look gray.

HOW MUCH DO CLOUDS WEIGH?

Because cloud droplets are so numerous that it takes several million of them to fill a cubic inch, you'd think that airplanes would get wet passing through clouds. The truth is that all these droplets don't add up to very much water. In a cloud, there's only a total of about 1 ounce of water in a space the size of the average 15-by-20-foot living room.

But clouds are pretty big, so if you could figure out a way to wring one out you'd end up with a fair amount of water. To obtain a rough measurement of the total weight of water in one of those puffy cumulus clouds, scientists estimate the size of the shadow the cloud makes on the ground when the sun is directly overhead. Say the shadow measures 1/2 mile square, and assume it is as tall as it is wide. Multiplying length times width times height to get cubic feet, then dividing by .01765 ounces of water per cubic foot gives you a total of a little under 1 million ounces of water, or about 58,000 pounds.

In a cloud, there's only a total of about 1 ounce of water in a space the size of the average 15-by-20-foot living room.

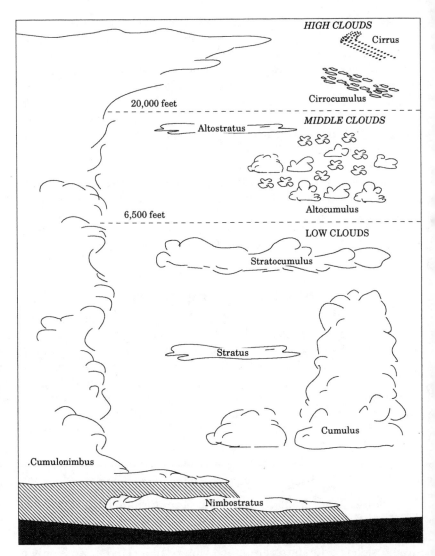

Labels in figure:
HIGH CLOUDS
Cirrus
Cirrocumulus
20,000 feet
MIDDLE CLOUDS
Altostratus
Altocumulus
6,500 feet
LOW CLOUDS
Stratocumulus
Stratus
Cumulus
.Cumulonimbus
Nimbostratus

YOU CAN'T TELL THE CLOUDS WITHOUT A PROGRAM

The key to using observation of the clouds to forecast weather is distinguishing the different kinds of clouds. Our system of classifying clouds was developed by a British pharmacist named Luke Howard in 1803. When he wasn't dispensing or manufacturing medications, Howard spent every spare hour observing what he called "the countenance of the sky." He decided to develop a system of classifying clouds according to their appearance and behavior. In order to affix names that were "worthy of notice," he used Latin, the language of scholarship in that day. Howard's system turned out to be so elegantly simple and useful that meteorologists still use it today.

Howard classified clouds into three basic groups:

- *Cumulus* (from the Latin word meaning "heap") clouds are the puffy individual clouds formed by rising vertical air currents.

- *Stratus* (from the Latin word meaning "widespread" or "layered") are the horizontal blankets of clouds or fog that cover most of the sky.

- *Cirrus* (from the Latin word meaning "a lock of hair") are the high-level, wispy strands of clouds.

To describe clouds that were in the process of producing rain or snow, he affixed the word *nimbus*, which is Latin for shower. Thus, a cumulus cloud that turns into a thundercloud is a *cumulonimbus* cloud, or a "heaped cloud that produces rain."

Howard also combined words to describe cloud combinations. For example, cumulus clouds that join together in a layer that covers the sky are *cumulostratus* clouds, while cirrus clouds that form a thin white veil high in the sky are *cirrostratus* clouds.

Sometimes low-level stratus clouds develop "hot spots" that rise to form puffy cumulus clouds above, which are called *stratocumulus clouds*.

Spending just a few minutes a day watching clouds over the course of a week or so will convince you of the accuracy and elegance of Luke Howard's basic system. Over the course of the last two centuries, meteorologists have added more names and prefixes to cover the many variations of the basic cloud types that are interesting to the serious student of weather. But learning to recognize and interpret the basic cloud types can make you a pretty canny weather forecaster.

WHAT YOU SHOULD KNOW ABOUT CUMULUS CLOUDS

Three types of cumulus clouds form in the lower part of the sky. Those fleecy, white *fair weather cumulus clouds* that drift across the bright blue sky on a fair day are the most short-lived of all clouds. They form when the sun heats the ground or pavement, which in turn heats air, which rises in a vertical column, and they are soft and puffy because their growth stops quickly. However, the wind blows the cloud away from the source of warm air, and it evaporates in just 10 to 15 minutes. Fair weather cumulus clouds don't produce precipitation.

One interesting fact about cumulus clouds is that they seldom form over the ocean or large lakes. The reason is that water doesn't absorb heat quickly enough to warm the vertical columns of air that cause these clouds.

In more humid weather, stronger vertical updrafts create *heavy cumulus clouds.* While these clouds are growing, they have a boiling appearance, as the sides appear to bulge out. The bottoms of these larger clouds are relatively flat and dark. Sometimes they build high enough to produce brief showers.

Cumulonimbus clouds are massive, cauliflower-shaped structures with flat, anvil-shaped tops. These monster clouds, dark and massive, produce heavy thunderstorms with strong rains and sometimes hail.

Cumulus clouds that form between 6,500 feet and 18,000 feet are called *altocumulus clouds,* while those that form at higher levels are called *cirrocumulus clouds.* Differences in wind speeds in two layers of air may give both a rippled, wave-like appearance, with patches of blue sky between the "waves." These clouds often appear 100 to 200 miles ahead of large weather systems that may bring precipitation.

WHAT IS A MACKEREL SKY?

Mackerel sky is an old mariner's term for altocumulus or cirrocumulus clouds with a rippled effect that makes them look like fish scales. As we just said, such clouds are a sign of an impending storm.

WHAT YOU SHOULD KNOW ABOUT STRATUS CLOUDS

Stratus clouds are those that form horizontal layers that cover all or most of the sky. *Low-level stratus clouds* tend to be thin, so the precipitation they bring is limited to drizzle or flurries. Stratus clouds that extend near or to the ground are called *fog.*

Cirrostratus clouds are translucent veils of white that float high in the sky, above 20,000 feet. They cause observers to see halos around the sun or moon. These clouds are a sign of an approaching warm front, the air of which has slid over the colder air to form this thin veil.

Altostratus clouds are white or gray layers of clouds that cover part or most of the sky. Although *alto* means "high" in Latin, they are really only the second-highest stratus clouds. These layers are thicker than cirrostratus clouds, but they often allow the outline of the sun or the moon to shine through. Altostratus clouds form as the front moves closer.

Nimbostratus clouds are low, thick, dark, threatening clouds that often produce steady rain or snow. They form when altostratus clouds thicken and lower as a front moves in. They often spawn small, fluffy dark clouds called scuds that float below the thick layer. Scuds are sure signs of approaching inclement weather.

Cumulonimbus clouds are massive, cauliflower-shaped structures with flat, anvil-shaped tops.

MORE ABOUT FOG

Fog is simply a cloud that touches the ground. Most fog is composed of water droplets, but in polar regions fog sometimes forms from ice crystals. Fog provides a fascinating glimpse of what it's like to be in a cloud, but it also can be extremely dangerous to all forms of transportation.

Fog generally forms under one of three different types of conditions. *Ground fog*, or radiation fog, tends to form on clear summer nights when the ground cools rapidly. The fog forms most readily in low-lying areas and valleys, where a gentle breeze cools air to the dew point by bringing it in contact with the ground, then trapping it as it condenses. This type of fog is thin and tends to burn off quickly when the sun shines.

Another kind of fog, called *evaporation fog,* tends to form over inland lakes and rivers in autumn when the air is cold and the water still retains warmth. Water evaporating from the warmer lake or river saturates the cooler air until the fog is formed.

The thickest and most persistent type of fog is *advection fog,* which occurs when warm, moist air is carried over a mass of colder water or air. For example, warm air from the Gulf Stream flows over the frigid Labrador Current near Newfoundland to form the famous Grand Banks fog, among the most persistent in the world. Off our West Coast, warm moist Pacific Air passes over the cold California Current to form the fog that often shrouds San Francisco.

WHAT IS DEW?

Dew is water vapor that is cooled by a cold surface and condenses. It tends to occur on clear spring or fall nights when the ground cools rapidly after a warm day but the moisture content of the air isn't high enough to form fog. Dew condenses on grass and plants, because hard surfaces such as dirt and pavement retain enough heat to cause vertical movement of air to carry the moisture upward.

Dew forming on cut grass can create a magical visual image. If you stand with your back to the sun in the early morning while the dew is still wet and shiny, you may see a distinct halo surrounding the head of your shadow. Some early religious folks used to believe this halo was a recognition of their own saintliness—in truth, it's an illusion caused when dew drops bend and reflect sunlight. But if the vision makes you feel divine, go ahead and enjoy it.

WHAT IS HAZE?

Haze also occurs when conditions aren't right to form a cloud. It results when there are lots of particles in the air, but the amount

If you stand with your back to the sun in the early morning while the dew is still wet and shiny, you may see a distinct halo surrounding the head of your shadow.

of moisture in the air is too low or the temperature is too high to form a cloud. If there is little or no wind to blow the particles away, sunlight can reflect off them to form haze.

Haze formed from particles emitted by motor vehicles and factories often blots the air in urban areas. But the air doesn't have to be dirty for this to happen. Haze caused by salt particles tossed into the air by waves can extend for miles over the seashore.

WHAT YOU SHOULD KNOW ABOUT CIRRUS CLOUDS

Cirrus clouds consist of ice crystals floating high in the troposphere. The light of the rising and setting sun reflecting off these thin, wispy, delicate clouds are often spectacular in color. Longer, feathery strands of cirrus clouds are called *mares' tails*, and they occur when ice crystals fall into slightly slower winds. Isolated cirrus clouds have no forecasting significance, but a sky full of these clouds is the first sign of an approaching warm front that may bring precipitation. Any light precipitation that falls from cirrus clouds evaporates before it reaches the ground.

Keeping company with cirrus clouds high in the troposphere are *contrails*, long white clouds formed from the moist exhaust of jet airplanes. Watching these contrails can provide a clue to upcoming weather. If the air above is very dry, the contrails evaporate rapidly. However, if the streams of clouds linger for an hour or more, the air above is damp, foretelling the arrival of a storm front.

MISTAKING CLOUDS FOR UFOS

Among the strange clouds that Luke Howard may never have seen are lens-shaped, or *lenticular clouds*. These clouds are formed when air rises to clear a mountain, then is blown downwind. The shape of these clouds, along with the iridescent light that they often reflect on moonlit nights, give them the appearance of flying saucers. Groups of these clouds floating along in formation have led to reports of a fleet of alien spaceships swooping down from the heavens.

Rarer phenomena that can also appear extraterrestrial are *noctilecent* clouds, strange formations in the mesosphere 50 miles above us, five times higher than any other cloud. These silver-white veils, which can be seen only in the dark sky after sunset, appear when the coldest part of the atmosphere drops to its coldest temperatures, about 225 degrees below zero Fahrenheit. Their strange light so high in the sky has also been interpreted as the light of alien ships.

HOW DO WE MEASURE THE HEIGHT OF CLOUDS?

The height of a cloud is the distance from the ground to its base. The height of the lowest clouds that cover more than half the sky is called the "ceiling," a calculation of great interest to pilots. A ceiling of zero means that the cloud heights are below 50 feet—in other words, fog has rolled in. An unlimited ceiling doesn't necessarily mean a total absence of clouds, but rather that clouds cover less than 50 percent of the sky.

WHAT'S THE DIFFERENCE BETWEEN PARTLY SUNNY AND PARTLY CLOUDY?

The U.S. Weather Service and other forecasters use a variety of terms to describe the sky above us, including the common and confusing "partly sunny" and "partly cloudy." Because the sky conditions are important to pilots, the Weather Service uses one terminology for aviation reports. This language is based on computing what percentage of the sky, rounded to the nearest 10, is covered by clouds:

Portion of sky covered	Description of sky
Less than 10%	Clear
10% to 50%	Scattered clouds
50% to 90%	Broken clouds
More than 90%	Overcast

In weather forecasts aimed at the general public, the terminology used is not quite so well defined:

Fair means that less than 40 percent of the sky is covered with clouds, with no fog or haze.

Partly sunny and *partly cloudy* can be used interchangeably when 30 percent to 70 percent of the sky is covered by clouds. Some weather people have a strong preference for one term; others use partly sunny when they feel the sun will predominate and partly cloudy when they feel there will be more clouds.

Cloudy or *mostly cloudy* are used when more than 70 percent of the sky will be covered by clouds.

A ceiling of zero means that the cloud heights are below 50 feet—in other words, fog has rolled in.

WIND: SETTING THE WEATHER IN MOTION

6

Anyone who saw pictures of the devastation unleashed on Florida, Louisiana, and Hawaii last August by hurricanes Andrew and Iniki clearly understands why ancient peoples considered strong winds to be the punishment of the gods. It seemed incomprehensible even to the relentlessly logical Aristotle that a force capable of uprooting trees and smashing buildings could be simply air in motion. Some who didn't believe that winds were created by angels flapping their wings or bellowing deities thought winds were the breaths of a living Earth.

The truth is that wind gives life to the Earth. If there were no winds, our planet would be a far different place. Instead of lush equatorial rain forests, all tropical lands would be deadly, barren deserts with daytime temperatures reaching upward of 130 degrees Fahrenheit. The vast interior of North America would be an equally arid but frigid desert uninterrupted by lakes, ponds, rivers, or streams. The New York harbor that has welcomed tens of millions of immigrants would be icebound year around, with a climate rivaling that of present-day Antarctica. It's doubtful that any complex life forms (including you and me) could have developed under these conditions.

WHAT IS WIND?

Wind is our term for the horizontal movement of air—the vertical movements of air we've talked about in cloud formation are called *currents*.

WHAT CAUSES WIND?

Wind is created by differences in air pressure between two air masses. Differences in air pressure are caused by uneven heating of the Earth's surface. As air warms, the molecules expand and rise, reducing the air pressure. Cold, dense air flows in to replace it, creating wind.

To picture how air molecules move from high pressure to low pressure, picture a seesaw with round ping pong balls (represent-

As this bit of videotape demonstrates, our on air coverage of Hurricane Gilbert was an "uplifting" expierience. (Don't worry, my feet never left the ground.)

ing air molecules) on each end. If the air pressure is the same, there's no movement and no wind. If the air pressure is lower on one end, the air molecules on the higher end role "downhill" toward it, creating movement. The greater the pressure difference (the steeper the slope), the faster the air molecules (wind) move.

To compute how fast a ball would roll down a hill, you would have to use formulas based on the weight of the ball and the angle of the slope. To forecast how strong winds will be, meteorologists have formulas that use exact differences in air pressure (the weight of the air) and the distances between air masses (the height of the slope) to compute a statistic called the *pressure gradient force.*

Slight differences in pressure produce a lower pressure gradient force, resulting in only gentle breezes. A good example is the breeze that develops near a large body of water. During the day, the land warms more quickly than the water, so the cooler air moves toward the land to create an onshore breeze. At night, the land cools more quickly, so the breeze turns around and blows offshore toward the warmer water.

When a large low-pressure system collides with a high-pressure system, the result is often gale force winds. The most destructive winds, those of hurricanes and tornadoes, result when air rushes

During the day, the land warms more quickly than the water, so the cooler air moves toward the land to create an onshore breeze.

toward the extremely low pressure at the eye of the storm.

FRICTION ALSO AFFECTS THE STRENGTH AND DIRECTION OF THE WIND

A ball will roll faster down a dirt slope than a slope covered with thick grass because it encounters less resistance. Similarly, the

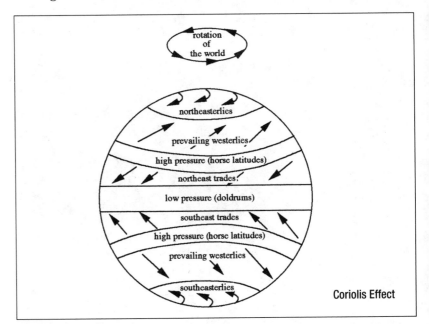

Coriolis Effect

less resistance offered by the surface, the stronger the winds. Wind encounters the least friction blowing over water. That's why ocean winds in the southern hemisphere, which has only 20 percent of the world's land area, regularly reach speeds of 100 miles an hour or more, far stronger than normal ocean winds in the northern hemisphere.

Winds also encounter less friction blowing over deserts, snow and ice, and flat plains than they do blowing over forests or hilly terrain. That's why farmers plant lines of trees as wind breaks to prevent winds from building to the point where their crops are damaged or soil is eroded.

THE SPINNING EARTH CURVES THE WIND

We don't notice that the Earth spins on its axis, because we're attached to it, along with our houses, automobiles, trees, mountains, and other physical features. But the atmosphere isn't attached to the ground, which is constantly rotating out from under it. If, though, the pressure gradient force directs the wind "downhill" on a straight line from air mass A to air mass B, B is moving by the time the wind gets there. So from our perspective on the ground, the wind seems to curve in the direction of the rotation.

If this seems hard to understand, imagine that you're riding on a carousel with a tennis ball in your hand. If you toss the ball straight up in the air, will you be able to catch it? Of course not, because you will have rotated part of the way around the circle by the time the ball lands behind you. To you and anyone else on the carousel, the path of the ball seems to be a curve. To an observer standing off the carousel, the ball's path seems to be straight up and down.

The principle that the path of any object set in motion on a rotating surface curves in relation to any other object on the rotating surface was mathematically proved by a brilliant French scientist named Gaspard Gustave de Coriolis. In his honor, we call this principle the Coriolis effect, and it has to be taken into consideration by anyone who launches anything up into the air. For example, gunners firing artillery shells long-range have to compensate by as much as a mile or more in order to hit the target. Calculations compensating for the Coriolis effect are programmed into the computers of guided missiles and jet airplanes.

The Coriolis effect doesn't have much influence on local wind patterns. But it profoundly influences the major patterns of wind flow around our globe, and it explains the patterns of air flow around high- and low-pressure systems.

GLOBAL WINDS: A ROAD MAP

Although our weather changes every day, many factors that affect the overall global climate stay pretty much the same over long periods. These include:

- The speed of the Earth's rotation
- The energy received from the sun
- The location of landmasses and oceans
- The size and location of the polar ice caps

Because of this consistency, our globe is ringed by bands of winds that generally blow in the same direction. These wind bands serve as Earth's "primary circulation," or the heating and air conditioning system that moderates our climate.

When we talk about these bands, we're going to concentrate on the northern hemisphere where we live. The wind systems in the southern hemisphere are mirror images of those in our half of the world—in other words, winds that blow in a westerly direction in

THE WORLD'S MOST FAMOUS WINDS

Few of us still believe that there are gods or other supernatural creatures that orchestrate the winds. Yet in all parts of the world there are wind patterns that are so familiar that it's natural to personalize them by giving them names. Following are descriptions of some of the most famous winds in the world.

• *Berg:* Hot and dust-laden winds that blow from the interior of southern Africa toward the coast, bringing several days of scorching temperatures.

• *Borasco:* Winds associated with violent thunderstorms, especially in the Mediterranean Sea.

• *Brick Fielder:* A hot, dry, dust-laden wind blowing from the deserts of Australia toward Sydney and the rest of the southern coast.

• *Buran:* A dreaded, violent, intensely cold wind that forms in Siberia and blows into southern Russia. It frequently carries heavy snows.

• *Chili:* A hot wind blowing from the deserts of North Africa and Arabia over the Mediterranean.

• *Chinook:* A very dry, warm wind that blows down the eastern slopes of the American Rockies. This wind can often raise temperatures as much as 40 degrees Fahrenheit in 15 minutes.

• *Doctor:* A British term for the cool sea breezes that blow over land in the tropics.

• *Fohn:* A general name for the dry, warm winds that blow down the lee side of mountain ranges (such as a "chinook"). The term was first applied to these winds that blow in Alpine valleys.

the northern hemisphere go the opposite way in the southern hemisphere.

HIGHWAY NUMBER ONE: THE TRADE WINDS

In planning his historic voyage in 1492, Christopher Columbus made a shrewd guess. He knew that Portuguese sailing ships sailing south toward Africa encountered prevailing winds blowing from the northeast. Columbus hoped that if he began his voyage by sailing south rather than due west, he would pick up these winds, which would propel him westward to the Far East.

He was half right; he didn't reach India, but he did find the winds he was looking for. He had discovered a wind band that soon became known as the trade winds, named for an archaic word meaning "course" or "track." These winds blow from the northeast toward the southwest from about 10 degrees to 30 degrees north latitude, a band that stretches from the northern tip of South America to a line that runs along the Florida–Georgia border and through New Orleans.

These winds result from a circulation of air that begins with the intense heating of the equatorial region by the sun, from about 10 degrees latitude north to 10 degrees latitude south. The heating causes the air to rise straight up, which means that there is almost no horizontal air movement, or wind, in this part of the globe. Sailors call this windless low-pressure belt the "doldrums."

The next movement of this air is determined by our old friend, air pressure. As we've discussed, cold air is denser and heavier than warm air, so gravity pulls it closer to the ground. That's why, at the surface, cold air has a greater pressure than warm air.

But at high altitudes the opposite is true. Because the cold air molecules are packed near the ground, there are more molecules in warm air in the upper atmosphere than there are in cold air. Therefore, at high altitudes, warm air has the greater air pressure and it heads "downhill" toward cold air. That's why, after our warm equatorial air goes straight up, it heads northward toward the poles.

Eventually, most of this air cools and sinks, causing a persistent band of high pressure around 30 degrees latitude north. Then some of the air is drawn back toward the low pressure at the equator, and it is this flow that creates the trade winds. Because the Earth spins faster at the equator, the wind seems to come from the northeast.

WHAT ARE THE HORSE LATITUDES?

You probably aren't going to be surprised that the horse latitudes are a large band of "stable" air (take a moment to groan) north of the trade winds. As the descending air is compressed by gravity, it heats up and dries out, clearing the skies. That means the weather in this belt is very dry and relatively windless. The great deserts of the northern hemisphere—the Sahara and Arabian in Africa, the Gobi in Asia, and the Mojavi and Great Basin in North America—lie along this belt.

• *Gharbi:* Winds from the Sahara Desert that pick up moisture and deposit it in the form of heavy rains over the northern and eastern Mediterranean. Sometimes the wind contains dust from the Sahara, causing "red rain."

• *Haboob:* Strong squall winds that produce extremely severe dust storms in the Sahara Desert.

• *Howling Fifties and Roaring Forties:* Sailors' names for the fierce winds that, unhampered by land or mountains, build up punishing strength in the middle latitudes of the southern hemisphere.

• *Levanter:* A strong east wind that frequently blows through the Straits of Gibraltar from the Mediterranean.

• *Mistral:* A north wind that brings strong cold, dry winds from the polar regions throughout Europe.

• *El Norte:* A flow of cold northerly air over the Gulf of Mexico and Central America.

• *Nor'easter:* A moderate-to-strong wind that brings cold and damp air from the northeast over New England coastal regions.

• *Santa Ana:* A Fohn-type wind, hot, dry, and dusty, that blows down from the mountains over the coastal areas of Southern California.

• *Sirocco:* A warm wind that usually sweeps northward from the Sahara Desert to the Mediterranean area. It often picks up moisture over the Mediterranean and arrives warm and moist on the southern coast of Europe.

• *Whirly:* A small but violent storm in the Antarctic.

• *Zephyr:* A term originating in the Mediterranean regions to describe a soft, gentle breeze.

Sailing ships were often becalmed for weeks in the waters along these latitudes. When a ship's food and water supplies dwindled, the captain was sometimes forced to order horses dumped overboard. The corpses of these horses floating on the calm waters led to the name "horse latitudes."

HIGHWAY NUMBER TWO:
THE MID-LATITUDE WESTERLIES

When it came time for Christopher Columbus to head back to Spain from his first voyage, he knew he wouldn't get far heading into the trade winds that had blown him along on the outward half of his voyage. So he sailed northward until he found some strong prevailing winds that flowed in the opposite direction. These winds are called the "mid-latitude westerlies."

They exist because not all of the warm air in the high-pressure horse latitudes flows back toward the equator. Some of it flows northward toward the poles. The Coriolis effect curves this air so that it flows from southwest to northwest from about 35 degrees north to about 60 degrees north latitude, a band that includes almost all of the United States and part of Canada. Then the air slams into cold air streaming southward from the poles and it's forced upward. It then flows back toward the horse latitudes at high altitude to complete the circulation.

This westerly flow is the reason almost all the weather systems in the United States move from west to east. It plays a vital role in creating our moderate, or temperate, climate, because it carries warm air northward and blocks the southward flow of frigid air.

HIGHWAY NUMBER THREE: THE POLAR EASTERLIES

Some of the warm air drawn upward to the top of the troposphere at the equator flows all the way northward to the poles. There it cools and sinks, creating high pressure. This cold, dense air then flows southward along the surface. Just as the trade winds are curved northeast to southwest by the Coriolis effect, so too are these polar winds, which we call the "Polar easterlies." Because temperature differences are less pronounced at these northern latitudes than they are farther south, the prevailing winds in this third circulation system tend to be weaker than the trade winds or the westerlies.

OCEAN CURRENTS: RIVERS OF WATER
DRIVEN BY THE WIND

Global winds and weather systems accomplish about two-thirds of the heat exchange that moderates our climate. The other third of the work is carried out by ocean currents, great rivers of water driven by the wind and by the forces of convection. Warm water from the tropics is blown by prevailing winds, circulating northward in a pattern determined by the Coriolis effect. When this water becomes cold, it sinks to the bottom and flows back toward the equator to be warmed again. These currents play a critical role in understanding the climate of the United States as well as the overall climate of the Earth.

The most important current, and the one almost everyone knows, is the Gulf Stream. This current begins when warm waters near the equator are carried northwest by the trade winds, following a course similar to that taken by Christopher Columbus. The water flows through the Caribbean into the Gulf of Mexico, then back out through the Straits of Florida. At this point it hugs the coast up to about Cape Hatteras, where it's propelled northeastward by the mid-latitude westerlies. In the middle of the ocean, the Gulf Stream branches: Some water turns directly east, some (the North Atlantic Current) flows toward Europe, and some continues in a more northern direction toward Iceland and Newfoundland. When the water finally turns cold, it sinks and heads back toward the equator along the coast of Africa.

The Gulf Stream has a profound moderating effect on the climates of the lands near which it flows. A city like London, which is as far north as Canada's Hudson Bay, would be ice-bound much of the time without the Gulf Stream; with the Gulf Stream, it has a climate more moderate than that of New York.

In the Pacific, on the other hand, the waters warmed in equatorial regions head west, away from the Americas. Then the mid-latitude westerlies produce a current that flows by Japan and back toward the Aleutian Islands. The water then sinks and flows back south along the Pacific Coast of the United States.

This pattern produces the cool, damp weather that characterizes much of the Pacific Northwest and northern California. A more positive effect is that Pacific hurricanes never threaten the U.S. coast—the cold water kills them.

A city like London, which is as far north as Canada's Hudson Bay, would be ice-bound much of the time without the Gulf Stream.

BOMBS OVER TOKYO: THE DISCOVERY OF THE JET STREAM

By the mid-19th century, the global system of surface winds was pretty well understood. But a critical bit of information about important upper-level winds was unknown until World War II, when American commanders decided to send a small group of bombers on a daring raid over Tokyo. After a long, lonely flight over the vastness of the Pacific, the pilots approached the Japanese capital at an altitude of about 30,000 feet to avoid detec-

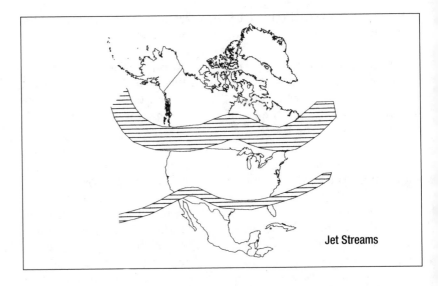

Jet Streams

tion and anti-aircraft fire. As they turned to make their bombing runs, the pilots suddenly noticed that their airspeed had soared to 450 miles per hour, far exceeding the rated capacity of their aircraft. As a result, most of the bombs landed far beyond their intended targets.

As the planes fled enemy territory, the pilots realized that they had stumbled onto a high-level wind roaring from west to east at speeds in excess of 150 miles per hour. Later flights confirmed that this river of air flowed all the way around the globe. We call this river the "jet stream."

The jet stream influences air navigation even today. A pilot headed from Chicago to New York can save 15 or 20 minutes' flying time and hundreds of gallons of fuel by slipping into the jet stream. Pilots going the other way are bucking the wind, leading to a longer and, to the airline, costlier flight.

WHAT PRODUCES THE JET STREAM?

As we've discussed, the strongest winds are produced by a clash of strong warm and cold fronts. The greatest temperature differences over the entire globe occur where the warm air pushed northward by the mid-latitude westerlies hits the cold air pushed southward by the polar easterlies. This intense clash produces a relatively narrow band of strong winds that blow at altitudes of 20,000 to 40,000 feet at wind speeds that range from 80 to 190 miles an hour. In the northern hemisphere, in the winter months, temperature differences between the warm air circulating north from the equatorial regions and the cooler air of the mid-latitude regions create a second, weaker jet stream that often flows across northern Mexico. In the summer, when the more direct rays of the sun eliminate temperature differences, this jet stream virtually disappears.

Because of the Coriolis effect, the general flow of the major jet stream is west to east. But it often dips to the south and rises to the north on its eastward path. In the summer, this jet stream is normally located well north into Canada and is relatively weak. However, in the winter, the temperature contrasts intensify, the jet stream picks up speed, and it often dips down into the United States.

Because the jet stream marks the sharp difference between warm and cold air, storms tend to track along its path like a bob-sled speeding along a run. When the jet stream dips southward, arctic air flows into the northern United States; when it meanders back northward, warmer Gulf air flows in behind it.

The jet stream, therefore, is one of the most useful factors in weather forecasting. It helps us predict the path of weather systems as well as changes in temperature.

THE LOCAL ROADS: THE WINDS WHERE YOU ARE

Understanding the global highways of winds helps us understand the movement of weather systems across continents. But in our everyday lives, we're affected a lot more by the day-to-day changes in the wind where we live. Learning about these winds can help us predict the weather and plan our activities.

To learn about the winds, we have to describe them accurately. We describe wind in terms of two variables, direction and speed.

WIND DIRECTION

In 50 B.C., Julius Caesar authorized payment of funds to a Greek architect named Andronikos for the design and construction of a "horologton," a magnificent eight-sided, 46-foot-tall white building in the heart of Athens. Why eight sides? The building was called the Tower of the Winds, and each side represented one of the eight directions from which the wind blew: north, northeast, east, southeast, etc. On each side was carved a sculpture that personified what the Greeks perceived as the characteristics of the wind that came from that direction. For example, North was represented by a man dressed in a warm coat; Northeast was a man carrying a jar filled with hail; West was a man carrying a flower pot; Northwest was a man carrying a firepot against the cold. On top of this majestic structure, which survives largely intact today, is the first known weather vane, in the shape of the sea god Poseidon.

Today, we still label the winds for the directions from which they come—e.g., a wind blowing from west to east is a "west" wind. Although the U.S. Weather Service sometimes divides the compass into sixteen directions (e.g., north, north-northwest, northwest, west-northwest, west, etc.), most weather people use the same eight directions as the Greeks.

The Greeks and Romans were also right about linking certain types of weather with wind directions. Bitterly cold arctic weather still flows from the northwest, and violent storms that occasionally bring hail blow from the northeast. More specifically, meteorologists keep records of wind direction and precipitation to develop patterns that are of great use in predicting the weather over the next 24 hours. For example, in one Connecticut city, a northeast wind means a 76-percent chance of precipitation in the next 24 hours in midwinter and a 66-percent chance in midsummer. With a northwest wind, however, chances of precipitation are only 34 percent in winter and 16 percent in summer.

HOW DO WE DETERMINE WIND DIRECTION?

We still use weather vanes, which are designed to point into the wind. In other words, if the weather vane is pointing northwest, the wind is coming from the northwest.

The only difference between us and the Romans is that our weather vanes are often linked to electronic instruments that record changes in weather direction. These are plotted by the points of a compass, with 0 degrees representing north, 90 degrees east, 180 degrees south, and 270 degrees west.

WHAT IS A WIND ROSE?

In the age of exploration, sailors also used compasses to record wind direction. In the 14th century, these compasses were often mounted on cards drawn with straight lines marking the four directions and a fleur de lis indicating north. This diagram became known as a "wind rose."

Today, a wind rose is a type of graph that shows at a glance the prevailing winds at any given location for a specific season of the year. It normally consists of eight lines drawn from the center of the compass rose toward the eight wind directions, with the length of each line increasing with the frequency of winds coming from that direction. In other words, if winds most commonly come from the northwest in a location, the line pointing northwest would be the longest. The points of all eight lines are connected to form a shape.

Meteorologists also plot wind rose graphs to show at a glance the speed of winds from each direction and the probabilities of precipitation with winds from each direction.

In the 14th century, compasses were often mounted on cards drawn with straight lines marking the four directions and a fleur de lis indicating north. This diagram became known as a "wind rose."

HOW DO WE MEASURE WIND SPEED?

We express wind speed in miles per hour or, for nautical or aeronautical purposes, knots. A knot is one nautical mile per hour, with a nautical mile measuring 6,076 feet, or about 10 percent longer than a statute mile. A 25-mile-per-hour wind is equivalent to a 22-knot wind.

Meteorologists use a number of different kinds of instruments call anemometers to measure wind speed on the ground. The most common type has rotating cups that spin as the wind catches them, with the rate of spinning indicating wind speed. Upper-level winds are measured by sending up a weather balloon, then tracking the speed of the balloon using radar.

ESTIMATING WIND SPEED CAN BE FUN

You may not have an anemometer in your pocket, but you can learn to judge wind speed quite accurately by observing the effects of wind on trees, water, or other objects around you.

You can get a rough estimate by looking at a flag. If the flag is limp, the winds are calm or nearly calm. At 10 miles per hour, the flag hangs about halfway between vertical and horizontal; at 20 miles an hour, it's about two-thirds stretched out; at 30 miles an hour, the flag streams out in a fully horizontal position.

You can obtain a more accurate idea by learning to relate what you observe to the Beaufort scale, a numerical scale for indicating wind speed devised all the way back in 1805 by Admiral Sir Francis Beaufort of the British Royal Navy. This scale, which gives a numerical 0–12 rating to winds based on speed, is so useful that the U.S. Weather Service still uses it today. (If only my career could last that long!)

In weather forecasts, you may hear wind speeds summarized in a one-word description:

Description	Wind speed in miles per hour
Light	1–7
Gentle	8–12
Moderate	13–18
Fresh	19–24
Strong	25–38
Gale	39–54
Whole gale	55–72
Hurricane	73+

BEAUFORT SCALE

Beaufort Number	Miles Per Hour	Effects On Land	Effects On Water
0	Less than 1	Smoke rises straight up. No perceptible motion of anything.	Sea like a mirror.
1	1–3	Smoke drift shows direction. Tree leaves barely move. Wind vane shows no direction.	Ripples with scale appearance. No foam crests.
2	4–7	Leaves rustle slightly. Wind felt on face. Vane moved by wind.	Small wavelets, crests appear glassy. Waves don't break.
3	8–12	Leaves and twigs move. Loose paper and dust raised from ground.	Large wavelets with crests beginning to break. Scattered white foam crests.
4	13–18	Small branches are moved. Dust and paper raised and driven away.	Small waves, becoming larger. More frequent white horses (white foam crests).
5	19–24	Small trees sway. Large branches in motion. Dust clouds raised.	Moderate waves; many white horses; possible spray.
6	25–31	Large branches move continuously. Wind begins to whistle. Umbrellas used with difficulty.	Large waves begin to form. White foam crests more extensive.

Upper-level winds are measured by sending up a weather balloon, then tracking the speed of the balloon using radar.

7	32–38	Whole trees in motion. Walking difficult.	Sea heaps up. White foam blows from breaking waves in streaks.
8	39–46	Tree twigs break. Walking progress slow.	Moderately high waves. Well-marked streaks of foam.
9	47–54	Slight structural damage.	High waves. Dense streaks of foam. Spray may affect visibility.
10	55–63	Exposed trees uprooted. Heavy structural damage.	Very high waves with long over-hanging crest. White appearance to sea surface. Visibility affected.
11	64–72	Widespread damage.	Exceptionally high waves. Sea completely covered with foam.
12	73+	Severe damage and destruction.	Air filled with foam and spray. Sea completely white with spray. Almost no visibility.

WHY WERE HURRICANE ANDREW'S AND HURRICANE INIKI'S WINDS SO DEVASTATING?

Wind moving against any surface creates pressure that isn't proportional to its velocity, but to the square of its velocity. That means that a 100-mile-per-hour wind is not 10 times as strong as a 10 mile an hour wind, but 100 times as strong. Hurricane Andrew's 140-to-160-mile-per-hour winds exerted pressures of about 75 pounds per square foot, six times the pressure of winds that just reach hurricane levels.

FRONTS AND STORMS: THE BATTLEGROUNDS OF WEATHER

To understand what's happening outside, we need to understand how our weather is affected by the movement and clash of air masses.

It would be very nice if the winds did their job of distributing heat and water vapor around the globe as neatly and quietly as a waiter in a fancy French restaurant delivers our food and beverages. Although I admit that violent storms make studying the weather more interesting, I simply don't enjoy forecasting or reporting hurricanes, tornadoes, crippling blizzards, or other turbulent WX events ("WX" is an abbreviation for weather). I'd much rather spend my mornings talking about brilliant sunshine and gentle rains.

But, unfortunately, the atmospheric waiters that deliver our weather are more like the Three Stooges, so our WX menu is a melange of everything from minor slips to major crashes and clashes. To understand what's happening outside, we need to understand how our weather is affected by the movement and clash of air masses.

AIR MASSES: THE ATMOSPHERE'S RESERVOIRS

There are certain areas of the world, such as the frozen tundras of the North and the warm waters of the oceans, where the weather is so stable that the mass of air above acquires uniform temperature and moisture content. The time required for these masses to form ranges from two or three days for air over very warm water to two or three weeks for air over dry land. These masses are like reservoirs because they hold huge quantities of air that have one of four sets of characteristics: warm and dry, warm and moist, cold and dry, or cold and moist.

Changing wind patterns occasionally break the dam that holds the air in place, allowing it to drift along with the winds. These oceans of air change the weather in the regions over which they move; for example, they bring cold arctic air to the southern United States or heavy rains to the arid Southwest. In turn their temperatures and moisture content are modified by the terrain over which they pass.

THE SEVEN SISTERS OF WEATHER: THE MAJOR AIR MASSES IN OUR PART OF THE WORLD

Our weather in North America is affected by seven major air masses. They are:

1. *Arctic Air Mass.* This mass forms above the snow and ice of northern Alaska, northern Canada, Greenland, the islands of the Arctic Ocean, and Siberia. This air is very cold (down to -60 degrees Fahrenheit in winter) and very dry. It produces little snow, except when it picks up moisture crossing a large body of water. This frigid air profoundly affects Canadian weather, but it does not often intrude into the continental United States.

2. *Continental Polar Air Mass.* This mass forms across the wide expanse from central Alaska to the prairies of Canada and

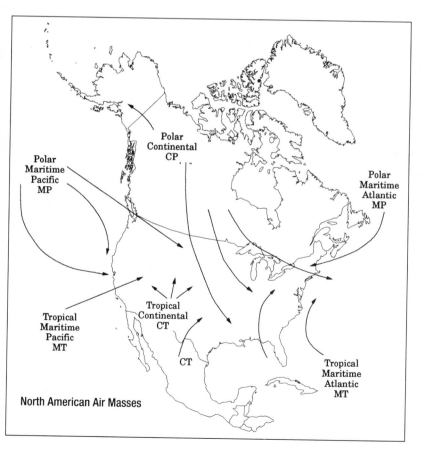

Polar Continental CP

Polar Maritime Pacific MP

Polar Maritime Atlantic MP

Tropical Maritime Pacific MT

Tropical Continental CT

CT

Tropical Maritime Atlantic MT

North American Air Masses

Hudson Bay to Quebec and Labrador. Like its cousin, arctic air, this huge body of air is cold and dry. It tends to bring clear skies and, in winter, frigid temperatures that can on occasion dip into the southern United States. Polar air carries only light precipitation, except for moisture picked up over the Great Lakes, which it dumps on the far shores.

3. *Maritime Polar Pacific Air Mass.* This air mass is created when cold air from Siberia drifts over the north Pacific Ocean, which produces cold, moist air. In winter it brings snow and rain to the West Coast from southern Alaska to southern California; in summer it carries low clouds, drizzle and fog.

4. *Maritime Polar Atlantic Air Mass.* This cool and moist air mass forms over the north Atlantic Ocean from Newfoundland to New England, bringing low-level clouds, drizzle, and fog, especially in spring and early summer. This mass often stalls over the East Coast, producing days of dreary weather.

5. *Maritime Tropical Atlantic Air Mass.* The warm waters of the Gulf of Mexico, the Caribbean Sea, and the Atlantic Ocean provide huge volumes of moisture, producing a mass of warm, moist air.

6. *Maritime Tropical Pacific Air Mass.* This warm and moist air mass forms in the warm Pacific from Mexico to Hawaii. In summer, this warm, humid air dominates the weather in the eastern half of the United States. In winter, it provides the moisture for heavy snowfalls on the Atlantic Coast.

7. *Continental Tropical Air Mass.* The deserts of northern Mexico and the southwestern United States produce this very hot and very dry air. It occasionally brings badly needed rain and moisture to the southwestern United States. When this air mass stagnates over the Plains states it can produce drought.

WHAT IS A FRONT?

Before satellites provided us with pictures of global weather patterns, meteorologists had to painstakingly assemble subtle clues in an attempt to determine how storms formed and moved. It wasn't until the early 1920s that a brilliant group of meteorologists in Bergen, Norway, deduced that the violent weather of the middle latitudes was caused by warm and cold air masses chasing each other around the globe. With World War I fresh in their minds, they pictured the collision of two air masses as a battle-

With World War I fresh in their minds, scientists pictured the collision of two air masses as a battleground of air, and they named the line along which the air masses met a "front."

ground of air, and they named the line along which the air masses met a "front."

WHAT IS A STORM?

By definition, a storm is any kind of weather disturbance, from a spring shower to a raging hurricane. But we weatherpeople and meteorologists tend to use the word *storm* to refer to major weather disturbances created when large masses of air are on the move.

SIMPLE BATTLES: FRONT MEETS FRONT

From the standpoint of military strategy, many World War I battles were a real snooze; two armies faced off against each other on a broad front until one was strong enough to push the other backward. Some confrontations between warm fronts and cold fronts are equally simple, producing predictable types of weather:

- *Warm front:* Warm air overrides cold air. Warm air is usually lighter and carries more moisture than cold air. Because cold air hugs the ground, the warm front gradually rides over it. The first warm air can contribute to the formation of cirrus clouds at high altitudes when the base of the front is as far as 500 or 600 miles away. As the front moves closer, the warm air cools on contact with the cold air, and water vapor condenses as clouds. Because the slope of the front is so gradual—the warm air can be as close as 3,000 feet above the Earth when the base of the front is 100 miles away—these clouds often produce steady precipitation falling over a long period.

As the front moves closer, the warm air cools on contact with the cold air, and water vapor condenses as clouds.

- *Cold front:* The air of an approaching cold front wedges underneath the warm air and lifts it. Because the front is so steep, this lifting often produces strong rising air currents that form thunderclouds. Locally heavy showers and, sometimes, hail and tornadoes can result. But these fronts normally pass through very quickly.

- *Occluded front:* A cold air mass and a warm air mass are stalled. In weather battles, just as in real battles, sometimes neither force can gain the upper hand. Meteorologists use the word *occluded,* which means "stopped" or "shut off from penetration," to describe this stalemate. The result is a mixture of warm-front and cold-front weather that can linger for days.

CHURNING STORMS: THE STORY OF HIGHS AND LOWS

A decade before satellite pictures gave us an alien's-eye view of

This satellite view shows high pressure dominating most of the country, while a low-pressure system covers the southeastern United States.

our planet, scientists at the University of Chicago concocted a brilliant experiment that showed how storms develop in the temperate zones that include most of North America. The key pieces of equipment in this experiment: a dishpan and a record turntable.

The experimenters rigged the pan with equipment that cooled it at its center (to represent the pole) and heated it at its edges (to represent the equator). They poured in about an inch of water (to represent the atmosphere) and added some aluminum powder so they could see water currents.

When the turntable was still, the water formed a classic convection current, moving upward at the heated edges, inward toward the cooler center, then sank and headed back toward the rim. When the turntable was rotated, the tracks of the particles neatly curved in response to the Coriolis effect in a pattern strikingly similar to the pattern of prevailing winds in our hemisphere.

Then the turntable rotation was increased to a speed comparable to the speed of the Earth's rotation. The circulation patterns near the edges and the center were virtually unchanged. But in the middle, a region comparable to the middle latitudes on Earth, dramatic changes took place. A heavy collection of particles formed a streak that looked like a river winding its way around the pan—a river that was the equivalent of the jet stream. The rest of the region was covered by a pattern of wavy lines all the way around. When scientists added dye to the water, they saw that underneath the wavy surface the water formed horizontal whirls and eddies that spun as they moved along guided by the "jet stream," or the waves of water above.

These same whirls and eddies form in the atmosphere above us. Meteorologist call them cyclones and anticyclones, and like the whirlpools in the pan, they result from the instability created by the clash of warm and cold air in the middle latitudes. While they can spawn devastating storms, they also serve as gigantic atmospheric mixers, blending warm and cold air.

WHAT IS A CYCLONE?

Ready for a riddle? Suppose you were kidnapped, blindfolded, hauled onto a plane, transported somewhere in the world, and locked in a bathroom. How could you tell what hemisphere you were in? (I know it sounds unlikely, but play along with me.)

Give up? You fill the bathtub with water and wait a half hour or so until it's absolutely still. Then you open the drain. If you're in the northern hemisphere, the water will swirl counterclockwise down into the drain; if you're in the southern hemisphere, the water will swirl clockwise. The reason: our old friend, the Coriolis effect.

Once again, the same principle holds true for air as it does for water. Because of the pressure gradient force, air is drawn from high pressure areas into low pressure areas. Under certain conditions that form when warm and cold air masses are touching or close, this air becomes unstable and starts to spin. In the northern hemisphere, the air circulating into a low pressure area rotates in a counterclockwise direction; in the southern hemisphere, air rotates in a clockwise direction.

These whirling low-pressure systems are called cyclones (from the Greek word kyklon, which means "coil of the snake"). Cyclones range in diameter from 100 to 2,000 miles. Because air drawn into the cyclone rises and cools, these systems tend to produce clouds and precipitation. The speed of the winds around the center depends on the temperature difference along the front and the pressure gradient force. Just as a figure skater spins faster when she draws in her arms, a cyclone's winds increase as its spin tightens. A hurricane is a particularly violent kind of cyclone.

A cyclone that forms in the warm waters near the equator is called a tropical cyclone, while a cyclone that forms anywhere else is called an extratropical cyclone. The energy provided by warm, humid air near the equator makes tropical cyclones (the strongest

Suppose you were kidnapped, blindfolded, hauled onto a plane, transported somewhere in the world, and locked in a bathroom. How could you tell what hemisphere you were in?

of which we call hurricanes) spin much faster than extratropical cyclones. As a result, low-pressure systems forming outside the tropics are much larger than tropical cyclones. Because they are so spread out, they also form fronts when they encounter a high-pressure system.

WHAT IS AN ANTI-CYCLONE?

Another kind of air movement results when air is drawn out of a high-pressure area. In the northern hemisphere, the Coriolis effect spins this air in a clockwise direction (opposite in the southern hemisphere). This type of system is called an anticyclone.

Anti-cyclones also average about 1,000 miles in diameter, and they are generally much larger than cyclones, or low-pressure systems. The air spun outward by the system normally falls as it spreads out. Warmed by compression, this air absorbs water droplets and dissipates clouds, bringing fair weather.

WHAT DIRECTS THE MOVEMENT OF FRONTS, CYCLONES, AND ANTI-CYCLONES?

Two major factors determine how and where air masses and systems move. They are the jet stream and permanent highs and lows

WEATHER'S ROLLER COASTER: THE JET STREAM

The flow of the jet stream provides a track for the weather in our part of the world. The simplest pattern and the least complicated weather occurs when the jet stream flows straight from west to east. Because the cold and warm air stay apart, this pattern tends to generate generally fair weather with few strong storms.

However, this stability doesn't last for long, because our atmosphere has to get back to its job of mixing warm and cold air. So the jet stream starts to undulate in a north-south direction. Southward dips are called troughs, and cold air from the north flows in to fill them. A trough in winter, for example, can bring freezing temperatures to the southeast United States. A rise to the north is called a ridge, and warm air flows in behind it. In the summer, ridges bring warm, moist Gulf air to the eastern half of the United States.

The contrast between the air in a trough and the air in a ridge tends to generate cyclones and anti-cyclones. But eventually the circular movements of these systems thoroughly mix the warm and cold air. With the temperature contrasts gone, the storms—along with the troughs and ridges—disappear and the jet stream flows straight west to east again.

The contrast between the air in a trough and the air in a ridge tends to generate cyclones and anti-cyclones.

PERMANENT HIGHS AND LOWS

The highs and lows that produce our daily weather are travelers, or migratory systems. However, there are four permanent systems—two highs and two lows—in our area of the world. The lows spin off weather systems, while the highs direct their movements. These are:

• *The Aleutian Low*: This huge system, which sits over the Pacific Ocean around the Aleutian Islands between Alaska and Siberia, is the world's major storm factory. It mixes the sharply

The lows spin off weather systems, while the highs direct their movements.

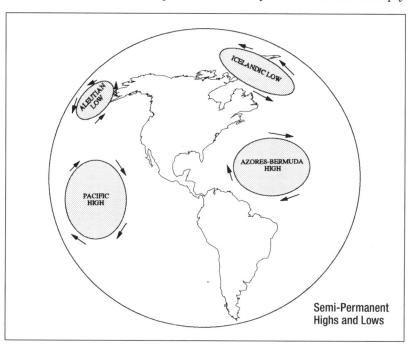

Semi-Permanent
Highs and Lows

different cold polar air with warm Pacific air, generating cyclones that are shipped off toward Canada and the northwestern United States.

• *The Icelandic Low:* This smaller sister of the Aleutian Low sits in the Atlantic Ocean off Iceland and serves as a magnet for cyclones that cross the western mountains into the eastern United States. It revives these storm systems and boosts them on their way to western Europe.

• *The Pacific High:* This large area is centered north and east of the Hawaiian Islands, although it migrates south in the winter and north in the summer. It directs weather systems coming from the Far East northward into the Aleutian Low.

- *The Azores-Bermuda High*: This companion system sits in the middle of the Atlantic, so strong that even the strongest hurricanes are unable to budge it. That's why hurricanes move westward through the Caribbean instead of heading northwest up the Atlantic. (I'll talk about this in more detail when we look at hurricanes.) When the high is particularly strong, it can block systems moving eastward, creating occluded fronts on the East Coast.

STORM TRACKS: BAD WEATHER ON THE MOVE

For much of the country, a system coming from the northwest brings fair weather, while a system coming from the southwest brings unsettled weather.

Cyclones and anti-cyclones can form anywhere and move in any direction. However, because of the relative permanence of the major air masses and major highs and lows in our part of the globe, they tend to follow common patterns called tracks. Shortly, we'll discuss the different types of storms and severe weather in detail and describe the patterns each tends to follow. But there are some general rules of thumb that provide good background.

First, it's useful to know that cyclones generally move in a northeast direction, while anti-cyclones generally move in a southeast direction. That means for much of the country, a system coming from the northwest brings fair weather, while a system coming from the southwest brings unsettled weather.

Second, storms need sources of moisture to continue to provide precipitation. For example, a low-pressure system that moves in off the Pacific through Canada or the Pacific Northwest will drop a lot of precipitation on the coast, but that precipitation will taper off as it moves over the Central Plains. However, if a trough in the jet stream swings that same low-pressure system down across the southwest and into Texas, it will pick up moisture from the Gulf of Mexico and produce major precipitation in the eastern half of the country.

Third, storms are weakened by mountains. Mountains lift a system, compressing it. The storm then slows—just think about how fast you can move while you're squatting—and drops heavy precipitation on the upslope side of the mountain range. By the time it comes down the other side, it's drier and weaker. Strong systems will regain strength as they move, while weaker ones will dissipate.

COMPLETING THE WATER CYCLE: THE STORY OF RAIN AND SNOW

I haven't completed a scientific study of the subject, but my experience tells me that more people watch the weather on TV to find out if precipitation is likely to fall the next day than for any other reason. Whether you're parents, picnickers, pothole repairers, or polo players, your plans for the next day are likely to be changed somewhat if rain or snow is expected.

It's only when precipitation is too plentiful or very scarce that we stop to think about its vital role in creating a livable environment on our planet. If air didn't contain water vapor, Earth would be as arid and dusty as Mars. (And I would be out of a job.) The way in which precipitation forms and falls is, in its way, one of the wondrous miracles of nature.

THE MYSTERY OF RAIN

Before people appreciated the miracle of rain, they had to solve a mystery: How did 1 to 15 million tiny cloud droplets come together to form raindrops? Microscopic water droplets tend to repel each other rather than be attracted to each other. The tiny ice crystals that make up most high clouds also repel each other.

Scientists struggled to find exactly what kind of atmospheric matchmaker was at work—until a brilliant German meteorologist named Alfred Wegener set his mind to the problem. Wegener, who later would revolutionize geology with his theory of continental drift (*e.g.*, if you have a few million years to wait, you'll be able to walk from San Francisco to Tokyo), was led to a conclusion by two facts. First, water droplets in the air don't always freeze at 32 degrees Fahrenheit. Instead, they are "supercooled" to temperatures of 20 degrees below zero or more, so they often coexist with ice crystals. Second, ice is less dense than water and has a lower pressure. So ice crystals attract water molecules.

Putting these two facts together, Wegener theorized that nearly all precipitation begins as ice, a theory confirmed by later

8

How do 1 to 15 million tiny cloud droplets come together to form rain-drops?

research. Ice crystals begin to form when cloud temperatures drop below 14 degrees Fahrenheit, which in summertime can happen in clouds two to three miles high. In the winter, ice crystals can form at much lower altitudes. These crystals begin to absorb water molecules from the supercooled water droplets. When they reach a certain weight, they begin to fall while continuing to attract water. At some point, almost all of them turn to snowflakes. If temperatures at lower levels are warm, these snowflakes turn to rain.

DO ICE CRYSTALS AND SUPERCOOLED WATER DROPLETS HAVE TO BE IN THE SAME CLOUDS?

No, not always. Sometimes ice crystals falling from higher clouds "seed" a lower cloud containing supercooled water. Precipitation results.

ARE THERE ANY EXCEPTIONS TO THIS RULE?

In meteorology there are always exceptions. In the 1940s, when airplanes began to carry instruments into high-level clouds all over the globe, scientists discovered that temperatures in clouds over the tropics never get cold enough for ice crystals to form. Since tropical rain obviously isn't a mirage, some other process must exist that allows rain drops to form.

The most obvious explanation was that raindrops form when water droplets collided with each other, in the same way the planet Earth grew as asteroids collided and stuck together. However, the number of collisions necessary for a million or more droplets to stick together would mean that raindrops would need months to form. The breakthrough came when scientists discovered that the water droplets in tropical clouds are many times larger than cloud droplets that form in areas out of the tropics. The reason is that the nuclei around which they form are salt particles blown into the air. If you've ever tried to use a salt shaker on a humid day, you know that salt absorbs water very easily. The huge water droplets in tropical clouds collide, clumping together until they form raindrops, then fall.

RAIN, SLEET, SNOW, ETC.: THE BASIC TYPES OF PRECIPITATION

The type of precipitation that falls depends on two factors: the temperature of the ground and the temperature just above the ground:

- Rain: Ground is above freezing and the air is above freezing.

- Freezing rain: Ground is freezing, air is above freezing.

Sometimes ice crystals falling from higher clouds "seed" a lower cloud containing supercooled water.

- Wet snow: Ground is above freezing, air is freezing.

- Sleet: Ground is freezing, a large layer of air is above freezing, and a narrow layer of air just above the ground is freezing.

- Dry snow: Ground is freezing, air is freezing.

HOW BIG ARE RAINDROPS?

Raindrops range from 1/100 to 1/4 of an inch in size. Any larger drops are split into two drops by air pressure as they fall.

WHAT SHAPE ARE RAINDROPS?

I feel like I'm telling you there's no Santa Claus, but you have to know—rain drops aren't that lovely tear-shape you always see in drawings. Instead, they look sort of like a hamburger, flat on the bottom and rounded on the top. The larger the drop, the more squashed the hamburger. (I can't believe I mustered up the courage to tell you that, but I relish the thought of it.)

HOW FAST DO RAINDROPS FALL?

The average-size raindrop falls at about 7 miles per hour (600 feet per minute) through calm air. The largest drops cascade at a top speed of about 18 miles per hour.

WHAT'S THE DIFFERENCE BETWEEN RAIN AND DRIZZLE?

There are a number of differences between drizzle and rain. First, drizzle drops are tiny, as small as 1/500 of an inch. The drops are dispersed evenly through the air—drizzle can look like fog, except that drizzle falls to the ground and fog doesn't. Drizzle doesn't come in showers but falls at a slow, steady rate that rarely exceeds 2/100 of an inch per hour.

We describe the intensity of drizzle in terms of visibility. "Light" drizzle occurs when you can see further than 5/8 of a mile; "moderate" drizzle produces visibility of 5/16 of a mile to 5/8 of mile; "heavy" drizzle means visibility of less than 5/16 of a mile. (No, I don't have the slightest idea why they measure visibility in 16ths of a mile—sometimes experts like things complicated.)

WHAT'S THE DIFFERENCE BETWEEN SHOWERS AND RAIN?

Showers are sporadic rainfalls that can vary in intensity from light to heavy in a few minutes. Showers, which fall from cumulus-type clouds, generally affect limited areas as small as a few thousand square feet. Sometimes you can see blue sky while a shower is falling from an isolated cloud overhead.

Rain falls continuously from thick, gray layers of clouds that cover the entire sky.

HOW DO WE MEASURE RAIN?

Amount of rainfall was one of the first accurate weather measurements, because it doesn't involved complicated instruments. However, measuring small quantities, such as .1 inch of rain, can be tricky. So most weather stations use a rain gauge topped by a funnel with a mouth exactly ten times the diameter of the collection tube. One inch of water in the collection tube means that .1 inch rain has fallen.

HOW DO WE DESCRIBE RAINFALL?

Rainfall is described in terms of the rate of fall in a given period of time:

- A *trace* describes rainfall too slight to be measurable.

- *Light* rain falls at a rate of less than .1 inch per hour.

- *Moderate* rain falls at a rate of .1 to .3 inch per hour.

- *Heavy* rain falls at a rate of .3 inch per hour or greater.

DO RAINMAKERS REALLY MAKE RAIN?

I've never admitted this on the air, but I have an infallible way to make it rain: It's called "scheduling a barbecue." No matter how perfect the forecast, come Saturday afternoon I'll be grilling hamburgers and hot dogs in my smoky garage while twenty people are playing volleyball in my living room. Some people have suggested that my damp social events result from some sort of curse placed on weatherpeople to repay us for the many events we have "ruined" for others.

If I could really make it rain, I'd be in great demand in many drought-stricken areas of the world. Since before the dawn of recorded time, people have been praying, dancing, or performing a wide variety of rituals to produce precipitation—and they still are. In 1992, tens of thousands of people rioted in Somalia because they believed that country's severe drought was caused by women wearing short skirts. (Hmmm, maybe that's why it doesn't rain often in Los Angeles.)

Anyway, the ultimate effectiveness of prayer and rain dancing is hard to determine scientifically. But a lot of supposedly "scientific" methods developed by self-proclaimed "rainmakers" have been downright frauds. One such wizard, Charles Hatfield, was immortalized in the famous 1956 Burt Lancaster movie, *The Rainmaker*. Hatfield proclaimed that he could attract rain clouds by boiling a mixture of secret chemicals on top of tall towers. After a number of widely publicized successes (and some very quiet failures), the city of San Diego agreed to pay him $10,000 to fill the nearly empty city reservoirs. Within hours after brewing up his stew, torrential rains began to fall. Streets were flooded, houses washed away, and a dam broke.

As a result, Hatfield was hit with a barrage of lawsuits. The California Supreme Court finally settled the issue by dismissing the suits on the grounds that rain is an act of God. Hatfield was thrilled—until the San Diego city council proclaimed that since rain was an act of God, the city didn't have to pay the rainmaker his $10,000.

Many other entrepreneurs have concocted rainmaking schemes, from firing rockets into clouds to aiming invisible beams. The results have been uniformly unreliable.

A government study showed that one small thunderstorm cloud held more than 33 million gallons of water.

CLOUD-SEEDING: THE ONLY SCIENTIFIC APPROACH

Methods of creating rain clouds are doomed to failure because of the immense volume of water vapor the clouds must contain. A government study showed that one small thunderstorm cloud held more than 33 million gallons of water.

A more practical approach is to encourage the formation of ice crystals in clouds that already exist. That goal was first accomplished in 1947, when three pounds of crushed dry ice were scattered over a cloud. The carbon dioxide crystals attracted supercooled water, forming snowflakes that melted and fell as rain. This technique, which provides the "seed" for the formation of precipitation, is called "cloud seeding."

Shortly afterward, cloud seeders began using silver iodide, a compound with an atomic structure very similar to ice crystals. Cloud seeding has proven to be of some usefulness in increasing the amount of precipitation that falls from existing clouds. But it is of no use in the dry air over drought-stricken areas.

WHAT IS A SNOWFLAKE?

In 1880, a young Vermont farmer named Wilson Bentley purchased a microscope and used it to examine a snowflake. What he saw through the eyepiece was an incredibly delicate, beautiful, six-sided structure formed from ice crystals. The sight was so breathtaking and fascinating, Bentley rigged up a camera to take a picture through the microscope.

Over the next 40 years, "Snowflake" Bentley, as he came to be called, took thousands of pictures of snowflakes. Eventually, he was able to list more than 80 different categories of snowflake structure. Yet over all those years, he never found two snowflakes that were alike.

Contrary to what we've always read and heard, scientists have never found a law of nature that prohibits two snowflakes from being identical. However, each snowflake contains about 180 billion water molecules that come together in such a random way under such a variety of conditions that observing two that are

In Hawaii, I take a few minutes to explain to viewers why the six-inch snowfall I forecast failed to materialize.

identical is extremely unlikely. Researchers have found that snowflakes formed at certain temperatures are often similar in appearance: At temperatures over 27 degrees Fahrenheit they are flat and hexagonal; between 23 and 27 degrees they tend to be needle-like; between 18 degrees and 23 degrees they tend to be hollow, prismatic columns. At lower temperatures, variety again prevails.

One characteristic of snowflakes is they are extremely good insulators. The reason: A lot of air is trapped inside the ice crystals that make up a snowflake. This insulating ability accounts for the eerie quiet that is characteristic of a snowfall. Snow cover is also a thermal insulator—during one Midwestern cold snap, the temperature on the surface of the snow was 27 degrees below zero, while just seven inches below the surface the temperature was plus 24 degrees. That's why Eskimos are comfortable in igloos.

WHAT'S THE DIFFERENCE BETWEEN WET SNOW AND DRY SNOW?

Subtle temperature differences in layers of air through which the snowflakes pass can produce many different kinds of flakes. The Eskimos, whose lives are profoundly affected by frozen precipitation, have names for several dozen different kinds of snow.

We only need to make a few such distinctions. Big, wet snow flakes result when individual flakes pick up moisture and start to stick together when they pass through a layer of above-freezing air. Sometimes the snowflakes melt entirely, then refreeze into pellets that attract a coating of ice crystals. This object that has an ice core surrounded by ice crystals is sometimes called "graupel." If the air is below freezing all the way down, snowflakes remain "dry."

WHY DOES SNOW OFTEN MELT AT FIRST, THEN START STICKING?

When a cold front comes through, the temperature of the ground often remains slightly above freezing while the air above cools. The first snowflakes melt as they hit the ground. But the evaporation resulting from the melting snow cools the ground. Eventually, the temperature drops to the freezing point and the snow sticks.

HOW FAST DOES SNOW FALL?

The rate of fall of snowflakes covers a vast range—some drift downward so slowly it can take them more than a day to reach the ground from 10,000 feet. Wet, heavier snowflakes can fall at a rate of three or four miles per hour.

HOW DO WE MEASURE SNOW?

Snow is the easiest of all meteorological measurements—weather observers just stick a yardstick or ruler in the ground in an area not affected by blowing or drifting.

HOW MUCH WATER DOES SNOW HOLD?

The rule of thumb is that 10 inches of snow is equivalent to one inch of rain. However, that ratio can drop as low as six to one with very wet snow. Meteorologists measure the water content of snow by collecting it on a flat surface, then melting it and measuring the run-off.

IS IT EVER TOO COLD TO SNOW?

Yes, it is. As you remember, cold air holds a lot less moisture than warm air. Air at 5 degrees Fahrenheit holds just .07 cubic inches of water vapor per cubic yard, 1/20 the water vapor held by

The Eskimos, whose lives are profoundly affected by frozen precipitation, have names for several dozen different kinds of snow.

a cubic yard of 86-degree air. That's why there is very little precipitation in polar regions. When the temperature is far below zero, the air's capacity to hold moisture is so low that human breath will turn to ice crystals and fall as snow.

WHAT IS "LAKE EFFECT" SNOW?

Cold polar air masses sweeping down from Canada contain relatively little moisture. They're often called "Alberta Clippers," because they move very quickly, depositing, at most, a couple of inches of snow.

However, these air masses do pick up significant moisture crossing large bodies of water, such as the Great Lakes. This moisture is often deposited as very heavy snow in a narrow band on the far side of the lakes. This lake effect is the reason cities such as Buffalo, New York, receive such high volumes of snow each winter.

WHAT IS A "NOR'EASTER"?

A "Nor'easter" is a storm that blows onshore off the Atlantic Ocean. Because it is laden with moisture from the ocean, nor'easters are responsible for the heaviest snows in New England and the Middle Atlantic states.

WHAT IS A BLIZZARD?

A blizzard is a severe winter snow storm characterized by:

- Low temperatures (10 degrees Fahrenheit or below)

- High winds (32 miles per hour or greater)

- Large volumes of snow that produce visibility of 500 feet or less.

The lake effect is the reason cities such as Buffalo, New York, receive such high volumes of snow each winter.

True blizzards are relatively uncommon; when they do strike, it is most often in Canada and the Northern Plains states. They are extremely dangerous to motorists and others without adequate shelter.

WHY DOES SALT MELT SNOW AND ICE?

Sodium chloride, or salt, prevents water from forming ice at temperatures of 20 degrees Fahrenheit or higher. Salt breaks up into sodium molecules and chloride molecules in water. The water molecules are more attracted to these sodium and chloride molecules than they are to each other, preventing them from forming ice crystals.

WHAT IS SLEET?

Many people use the word *sleet* when referring to a mixture of rain and snow. But the U.S. Weather Service uses the word to indicate raindrops that freeze into ice pellets just before they hit the surface.

WHAT IS FREEZING RAIN?

Freezing rain is precipitation that hits the ground as water, then freezes. The most damaging form is called "glaze" ice, which forms when raindrops shatter upon impact before freezing. This forms a heavy, impenetrable sheet of ice on roads, tree limbs, power lines, and other objects. The result is the most hazardous of all winter conditions.

"Rime" ice, on the other hand, forms when the raindrops hit and freeze unshattered. This forms very porous ice, like that which accumulates on the inside of a freezer.

THUNDERSTORMS: NATURE'S SOUND AND LIGHT SHOW

9

The Greeks went so far as to fence off spots that had been struck by lightning, so man would not tread on ground consecrated to the gods.

Thunderstorms have been the most awe-inspiring and fearsome weather events since prehistoric times. The pantheons of early civilizations were dominated by powerful gods whose voices thundered in rage as they wielded fiery fingers of lightning. These gods included the Greek god Zeus, the Roman god Jupiter, and the Norse god Thor. The Greeks went so far as to fence off spots that had been struck by lightning, so man would not tread on ground consecrated to the gods.

We may not believe in Zeus anymore, but most of us still fear thunderstorms—and with good reason. Thunderstorms spawn flash floods, lightning, and tornadoes, the three leading causes of weather-related death and destruction in the United States. Unlike hurricanes and blizzards, the paths of which are predictable, thunderstorms can turn severe with little warning, bringing destruction more terrifying because of its randomness.

Yet, they have benevolent as well as violent consequences. They provide as much as 80 percent of the rainfall during the growing season across the Great Plains and the Midwest. Each year, lightning produces, by electrically breaking down the nitrogen and oxygen in the air, more than 100 million tons of nitrogen compounds that act as valuable fertilizing agents in the soil on which they fall. In fact, many scientists believe that lightning triggered the chemical reactions in sea water that initiated life on Earth.

WHAT IS A THUNDERSTORM?

One thing I like about the weather is that many of the terms are easy to understand. A thunderstorm, for example, is simply a storm that produces visible lightning and audible thunder. Generating lightning and thunder is a process requiring an enormous amount of energy, energy which is built up in cumulonimbus clouds—heavy, towering, mountainous masses that can reach heights of 60,000 feet. More than 16 million thunderstorms form during the course of an average year. At any given point on an average day, 1,800 thunderstorms rage somewhere in the world, producing 6,000 lightning flashes per minute.

Most thunderstorms generate heavy rains and sometimes hail. In very dry regions, however, precipitation falling from a thunderstorm may evaporate before it hits the ground. These "dry" thunderstorms are called virgas.

WHAT CAUSES THUNDERSTORMS?

Most of the world's most severe thunderstorms could have the phrase "Made in America" stamped on them. That's because the geography of the United States east of the Rocky Mountains is the world's best breeding ground for heavy-duty boomers. The basic ingredient in the creation of a thunderstorm is a warm, moist air mass, and the humid tropical air that flows over the eastern and central United States from the Gulf of Mexico, the Caribbean, and the Atlantic Ocean around Bermuda during the spring and summer meets this requirement perfectly. In contrast, Pacific air that flows onto land is normally cool, which is why the western states average fewer than 20 days with thunderstorms per year.

Thunderstorms occur when this warm, moist air becomes unstable and is forced upward into the cooler atmosphere. The temperature drops about 1 degree Fahrenheit for every 300 feet the air rises. At some point, the air cools to the dew point, where moisture condenses into clouds of liquid droplets, for the same reason that mist forms on the outside of a glass of ice water on a humid day. The bottom of the clouds forms about 250 feet above the point at which water vapor starts to condense.

As anyone who puts a pot or kettle on the stove realizes, it takes considerable energy to turn water into steam. When water vapor condenses, that considerable energy is released in the form of heat. That heat pushes the air higher and higher. Tiny droplets merge into larger droplets, which may freeze into ice crystals at higher altitudes. Finally, the force of gravity overcomes the forces driving the warm air upward, and the moisture falls. Any ice crystals melt on the way down as heavy rain hits the ground. At its peak, a thunderstorm is like a two-lane highway, with updrafts feeding warm, moist air into the storm and a downdraft of cooled air and precipitation falling. Eventually, the downdrafts choke off the updrafts, and, with no new moist air as "fuel," the thunderstorm ends.

There are three basic types of conditions that produce the instability that brings about thunderstorms:

- "Air mass" thunderstorms are common late-afternoon
  occurrences in hot, sticky weather. Like water in a
  tea kettle, the warm air near the ground is confined

Thunderstorms occur when warm, moist air becomes unstable and is forced upward into the cooler atmosphere.

by a blanket of cooler air above. Intense sunshine heats the air, building up pressure. By late in the day, the air finally "boils," breaking through the blanket of cool air to rise, form clouds, and eventually create a thunderstorm. Such thunderstorms occur almost every afternoon on the Gulf Coast of Florida.

- "Frontal" thunderstorms take place when a cold front collides with a warm front. Because cold air is heavier than warm air, it acts like a wedge, driving underneath the warm air and mechanically forcing it upward. Frontal thunderstorms tend to be more violent than air mass thunderstorms because of the greater temperature difference between cold and warm air. Cold fronts moving down from Canada and colliding with warm, moist Gulf air over the Great Plains and the Midwest spawn especially severe thunderstorms and more than half of the world's tornadoes.

- "Mountain" thunderstorms form because the air around elevated peaks is warmer than the air over valley areas at the same level. Afternoon breezes that flow up the sides of mountains help produce the updrafts that cause thunderstorm formation. Such storms are common in the Rocky Mountains.

Any kind of thunderstorm can generate gusts of wind that can trigger additional thunderstorms up to 100 miles away. That's why thunderstorms often occur in lines called squall lines.

WHAT PART OF THE COUNTRY HAS THE MOST THUNDERSTORMS?

The Gulf Coast of Florida around Tampa and St. Petersburg leads the nation in boomers, with thunderstorms occurring an average of 130 days per year. That same warm, humid Gulf air produces thunderstorms 80 to 100 days a year on the rest of Florida's Gulf Coast as well as the Gulf areas of Alabama and Mississippi. Much of the remainder of Mississippi and Alabama, as well as most of Georgia and Louisiana, record 60 to 80 days of thunderstorms. The midwestern Corn Belt and the Great Plains states experience more than 50 days of thunderstorms, while the middle Atlantic, New England, and Great Lakes states have 20 to 40 per year. The Pacific Coast states experience only 5 to 10 thunderstorms a year, while Alaskans hear thunder and see lightning only once every 3 to 5 years.

Any kind of thunderstorm can generate gusts of wind that can trigger additional thunderstorms up to 100 miles away.

HOW LONG DO THUNDERSTORMS LAST?

The average thunderstorm lasts 25 to 40 minutes. The heaviest rain falls about two or three minutes after the first drops reach the ground, then begins to taper off five to 15 minutes later. The amount of water released can be enormous—averaging 500,000 tons in a typical storm. Especially vicious are rarer thunderstorms called supercells, which can last up to several hours as they travel more than 200 miles.

WHAT ARE SUPERCELL THUNDERSTORMS AND WHY ARE THEY SO DANGEROUS?

Supercells are the most powerful and longest-lasting thunderstorms. They form under a complex combination of conditions that occasionally occur when a strong cold front slams into very warm, humid air. As the cold air pushes the warm air upward, upper-level winds blowing in different directions cause the air to begin to spin. This spiral movement of air inside of a thunderstorm is called a mesocyclone. The diameter of a mesocyclone averages 10 miles, but can extend up to 250 miles.

The intense updraft of air caused by the spinning center produces downdrafts that clear the skies around the storm. That's why a supercell thunderstorm appears from a distance as a gigantic mountain of clouds amidst surrounding blue skies. Water vapor condensing as it is pulled into the mesocyclone often produces a "wall" cloud, which makes the bottom of the thunderstorm cell look flat.

Supercell thunderstorms are especially dangerous because they often spawn strong tornadoes, spiral currents of air that tighten and intensify as they reach toward the ground. Because the temperature contrast between cold Canadian air and warm humid Gulf air is most intense in spring and early summer, more supercell thunderstorms and more strong tornadoes occur in April, May, and June.

Supercell thunderstorms are especially dangerous because they often spawn strong tornadoes.

WHAT TIME OF DAY DO THUNDERSTORMS OCCUR?

Most people tend to think thunderstorms are most likely to occur just as all the food for the picnic is spread out on the blanket. The truth is, most local air mass thunderstorms occur in late afternoon and early evening when people are most likely to be sitting down to eat. Frontal thunderstorms can occur any time of day or night, although they are most severe in late afternoon or early evening. Thunderstorms forming over the Rocky Mountains during the day can drift over the Great Plains to cause evening or nighttime storms.

WHEN DO THUNDERSTORMS CAUSE FLASH FLOODS?

Flash floods can be produced by especially torrential rains called "cloudbursts." These occur when raindrops accumulating in thunderclouds are held aloft by strong updrafts of air. When the updrafts are finally shut off, the water cascades to the ground in a torrent like the bursting of a dam.

WHY ARE THUNDERSTORMS DANGEROUS TO AIRCRAFT?

Although some plane crashes have been attributed to lightning, electrical discharges aren't the biggest hazard to aviation. Instead, the biggest cause of crashes from storms is wind shear or microbursts, sudden, violent winds that can plunge downward at speeds of up to 200 miles per hour. A microburst is a downdraft that results when dry air enters a thunderstorm either from below or from a high-altitude wind. The thunderstorm cools the air, making it so heavy that it blasts downward. Wind shear can fell planes as well as cause tornado-like damage on the ground.

An even rarer form of violent wind is a heatburst. These are created when molecules of air in a storm are compressed so tightly that the friction creates intense heat as the air plunges to the ground. Thermometers in the path of heatbursts have reportedly reached momentarily high temperatures of 140 degrees Fahrenheit.

HAIL—HEFTY SNOW?

As we discussed previously in this book, water droplets in moist air become ice crystals as the air rises. In cold weather, these ice crystals join together to fall as snowflakes. In warm weather, the ice crystals melt on the way down to fall as rain.

Hail forms when nature catches these ice crystals in a kind of atmospheric trampoline. In some thunderstorms, the ice crystals that begin to melt in nonfreezing air are thrown back up into freezing air by updrafts and acquire another layer of ice. These updrafts can continue to bounce the ice crystals back and forth between freezing and nonfreezing air as they add layers like an onion. When they reach a diameter of about 1/5 of an inch, they are considered to be hail.

The stronger the winds blowing upward, the larger the hailstones grow. Eventually, the hailstones become heavy enough for gravity to overcome the force of the wind, and the stones fall to the ground through the thunderstorm in a column known as a "hailshaft." The ground area swept by the hailshaft is known as the "hailstreak." Hailstreaks normally vary from 100 feet to 2 miles wide, and average 5 miles in length. But giant storms have left swaths of hail 50 miles wide and 200 miles long.

The conditions that cause hailstones are more common in "Hail Alley," the midwestern and Plains states east of the Rocky Mountains, where the temperature contrast between cold fronts and warm fronts is more extreme. The hailstorm capital of the United States is Cheyenne, Wyoming, where nine or 10 hailstorms occur in an average year. On the other extreme, Florida has one of the lowest incidence of hailstones because its numerous thunderstorms are primarily of the air mass type.

Hailstones are seldom larger than marbles. But golf-ball-size hail is not rare in some parts of the midwestern United States. The largest hailstone ever officially measured in the United States, which fell on Coffeyville, Kansas, on September 3, 1970, weighed 1.67 pounds and measured 17.7 inches in circumference—about the size of a cantaloupe. There are lots of reports of even larger stones falling in the United States and in other parts of the world, but none have made it to the scale.

In the Great Plains, hailstorms have sometimes been so severe that highway crews with snowplows have had to be dispatched to clear the roads. A storm in southeastern Kansas in June 1959 left an accumulation of hail 18 inches deep over a 15 square mile area. On September 5, 1898, an incredible hailstorm in northwestern Missouri left hail that lasted for 52 days—on October 27, there was still enough left unmelted for residents to use in making ice cream.

Many deaths from hail have been recorded in densely populated areas of China and India. The worst disaster was caused by baseball-size hail that killed 246 people in northern India in 1888. The U.S. Weather Service has recorded two deaths by hail: a 39-year-old farmer killed in a Lubbock, Texas, field in May 1939, and an infant killed in its mother's arms in Fort Collins, Colorado, in July 1979.

The costliest hailstorm in United States history hit Denver, Colorado, on July 11, 1990, when a rain of golf-ball-size stones caused $700 million in damage.

The worst disaster was caused by baseball-size hail that killed 246 people in northern India in 1888.

WHAT CAUSES LIGHTNING?

I'm often asked, What causes lightning?, and I have to answer that I'm not really sure. But I'm not the only one who's in the dark. Even scientists do not completely understand the complex reasons why the friction resulting from the interaction of wind, water droplets, and ice particles causes separation of positive and negative electrical charges inside a cloud and on the ground. What we do know is that lightning results when electricity travels between areas of opposite electrical charges within a cloud, between two clouds, or about 20 percent of the time, between a cloud and the ground.

I'm glad I don't have to pay the electric bill for lightning, because the current in just one bolt is so enormous a storm could bankrupt even Ross Perot. Measurements have been recorded of bolts containing up to 345,000 amperes, enough electricity to service 200,000 homes. Pressure of the electricity in lightning can exceed 15 million volts. A single thunderstorm can produce continuous releases of energy greater than 1 million kilowatts.

ANATOMY OF A LIGHTNING STROKE

The discharge of lightning begins when a mass of negative ions builds up so much energy that it overcomes air's normally high

This photo dramatically illustrates the brilliant flash called the *return stroke*.

resistance to electric current. A channel of electrons a few inches in diameter (a "leader") forces its way downward in a series of steps about 150 feet long. This motion is the reason lightning looks jagged instead of straight.

When the leader nears the ground, it draws a "streamer" of positive electrons toward it, normally through something high, such as a tree or a lightning rod. When the two meet, they form a pencil-thin path for electric current to flow from ground to cloud. The lightening begins at the cloud, shoots down then back up again—like an electric circuit.

A microsecond after this path is formed, an intensely brilliant flash we call lightning surges *from ground to cloud* along the path created by the streamer. This flash, called the "return stroke," is the light we actually see. The wave of positive ions traveling upwards moves at 60,000 miles per second, about one-third the speed of light. Several waves of electricity can make the round trip in less than one second, which is why lightning often seems to flicker.

CAN LIGHTNING STRIKE TWICE IN THE SAME PLACE?

Lightning not only can strike twice, it often does. For example, the top of the Empire State Building has been struck a dozen times in a single storm and as often as 500 times in a year. Lightning detection systems have recorded an average of 40 million cloud-to-ground strikes annually, an average of 13 for every square mile in the United States each year.

DESCRIBING LIGHTNING

The following terms are used to describe lightning:

• "Streak" lightning is the ordinary zigzag bolt from cloud to ground.

• "Heat" lightning is streak lightning that's so far away thunder can't be heard.

• "Fork" lightning is a bolt that seems to break into several "fingers" that hit the ground at the same time.

• "Ribbon" lightning is streak lightning that looks billowy because the channel is blown sideways by the wind.

• "Sheet" lightning is a diffused white glow caused by the diffusion of many strokes of lightning in distant clouds.

• "Ball" lightning has been described as a pear-shaped ball of reddish or whitish light that floats horizontally before exploding. This effect has often been reported by observers but has not been confirmed by photographic evidence.

The top of the Empire State Building has been struck a dozen times in a single storm and as often as 500 times in a year.

WHAT ARE THE CHANCES OF BEING STRUCK BY LIGHTNING?

About one in every 500,000 people is killed by lightning in the United States each year, and about one in 125,000 is injured. Despite these long odds, one very unlucky Virginia park ranger named Roy C. Sullivan was struck by lightning eight times before his death (from natural causes) in 1982. He lost his big toe in 1942, his eyebrows in 1969, and his hair was set on fire twice. Only slight burns resulted from his other accidents.

Florida, which experiences more thunderstorms than any other state, has also recorded the greatest number of deaths by lightning over the last five years. However, western states with large flat open areas of land, such as New Mexico, Colorado, Montana, Wyoming, and the Dakotas, have the highest per-capita rates of death by lightning.

WHAT CAUSES THUNDER?

Until I became a weatherman, I thought thunder was the sound of dwarfs bowling in the mountains. Now I know thunder is caused by lightning. As it passes through, lightning heats the air to a temperature of 50,000 degrees Fahrenheit, five times the temperature of the surface of the sun. This heat causes the air to expand with an explosive force that produces the loud sound we call thunder. Thunder can be heard as far as 15 to 18 miles from the lightning bolt.

COMPUTING THE DISTANCE TO LIGHTNING STRIKES

Thunder and lightning occur at the same time. But light, which travels 186,000 miles per second, reaches your eye almost instantaneously, while sound, at a pokey 1,100 feet per second, takes a much longer time to reach your ears. To get a rough idea of the distance between you and the lightning strike, count the seconds from the time you see the flash to the time you hear the thunder. Every five seconds is a distance of about 1.2 miles.

Because of the relatively slow speed of sound, distant thunder sounds different from that created by nearby lightning. Thunder is produced by a series of explosions that occur as the electrical charge travels from ground to cloud. If you're close to the lightning, the sound reaches you quickly as one sharp crack. However, distance separates the sounds into a longer rumble.

PROTECTING YOURSELF FROM LIGHTNING

Common sense could prevent almost all deaths from lightning. Everyone should understand that all thunderstorms are potentially dangerous, because there is absolutely no current method of predicting if a specific storm will generate a few lightning bolts or hundreds of lightning bolts. So don't wait until the first lightning strikes—seek cover when the sky starts to darken.

Outside, never take cover under a tree, for the obvious reason that tall objects are the best way for a streamer of positive ions to

As it passes through, lightning heats the air to a temperature of 50,000 degrees Fahrenheit, five times the temperature of the surface of the sun.

reach the negatively charged leader. Don't ride a bike, push a lawn mower, ride a tractor, or wield a rake or golf club or any other object. If you can't make it inside, lie flat in any spot lower than the rest of the terrain.

If you're in a vehicle, stay there. Cars, trucks, vans, or buses provide excellent protection. Don't try to leave until the storm is over, because you're in danger when you're touching the vehicle and the ground at the same time.

Inside, don't use the phone, take a shower, or hold an electrical appliance. Lightning that strikes a building can travel through the telephone wires, plumbing system, or electrical wires.

TORNADOES

10

A tornado is the most violent of all the Earth's storms, with winds that can exceed 300 miles an hour producing devastating destruction and death in its narrow path.

If a hurricane is the Operation Desert Storm of weather, bringing dangerous winds and rains to a huge area, a tornado is a cruise missile. A tornado is the most violent of all the Earth's storms, with winds that can exceed 300 miles an hour producing devastating destruction and death in its narrow path. While hurricane winds can bend and break trees, tornadoes can uproot them and fling them hundreds of yards in the air. Also sucked up into the vortex of tornadoes have been automobiles, buses, even railroad cars. The fear inspired by tornadoes is well justified by the terrible risk they pose to life and property.

WHAT IS A TORNADO?

A tornado is a violently rotating column of air that stretches from the base of a cloud to the ground. The word *tornado* comes from the Spanish *tornado*, the past participle of the verb that means "to turn." The devastating force of a tornado comes from the increasing speed with which air "turns" as it tightens into a funnel, in the same way that a figure skater speeds up her spin by pulling her arms to her chest. (The fancy name for this principle, if you're interested, is "conservation of angular momentum.") We can see this air spinning as it drops from the cloud toward the ground because low pressure causes water vapor to condense, making the tornado look like a funnel made of clouds. When the tornado reaches the ground and sucks up dirt and rocks, it often turns black; if it sucks up red clay, it can have a red appearance.

WHAT CAUSES TORNADOES?

We know a lot more about the conditions under which tornadoes occur than we do about what exactly triggers a tornado. Almost all tornadoes occur when the air temperature is above 65 degrees Fahrenheit and the dew point is more than 50 degrees Fahrenheit. Most tornadoes are associated with the conditions that spawn severe thunderstorms, which occur either when a warm, moist air mass is heated to the point where air starts to rise or when a cold air mass encounters warm, moist air along a front.

Air mass thunderstorms can spawn tornadoes when the upward

pull of air is especially rapid, which is why Florida annually records the largest number of these storms. Fortunately, nearly all of these tornadoes are weak and short-lived.

Almost all "killer" tornadoes result from some special conditions that can occur along a frontal boundary between cold and warm air. Normally, the cold air wedges under the warm air, starting a vertical current that builds into a thundercloud as high as 60,000 feet. But sometimes the cold air mass moves so quickly that friction holds back the air at the surface, and a tongue of cold air reaches out to put a "cap" on the warm air at an altitude of 1,000 to 2,000 feet. This is a very unstable condition. If upper-level winds are strong, the cold air and warm air are swirled together, forming the mesocyclone we talked about when we discussed thunderstorms. The twisting air in the mesocyclone can in turn create smaller vortexes of spinning air that grow faster and more furious until they form funnel clouds that reach downward out of the cloud. When a funnel cloud touches the ground, it becomes a tornado.

These conditions are often associated with massive thunderstorms that produce intense hail and almost continuous lightning. Tornadoes often occur after the heaviest downpour of rain from a thundercloud. Some meteorologists speculate that downdrafts of colder air near the rear of a thundercloud help to guide the funnels to the ground.

The whirling winds of a massive hurricane often spawn tornadoes when the hurricane moves onto land. In 1967, Hurricane Beulah unleashed 115 tornadoes as it moved off the Gulf over Texas. Hurricane-produced tornadoes, however, are generally small and very short-lived.

In 1967, Hurricane Beulah unleashed 115 tornadoes as it moved off the Gulf over Texas.

WHERE DO TORNADOES STRIKE?

America is number one in many categories, but one such distinction we're least proud of is our leadership in the number of tornadoes per year. In fact, almost three-quarters of the world's tornadoes occur in the continental United States.

Tornadoes have touched down in all 48 contiguous states, but, like thunderstorms, they are rare west of the Rocky Mountains. Because tornadoes develop on the border between warm and cold air, the area having the most frequent tornadoes changes with the seasons. In January and February, tornado activity is limited to the states bordering the Gulf of Mexico. In March and April, tornadoes are most likely in the lower Mississippi Valley and the lower part of the Central Plains. From May through September, the upper Midwest from the Rockies to the Ohio Valley is the prime target. Then the area most likely to have tornadoes moves southward with the cooler temperatures until it's back in the Gulf States in November and December.

The area punished most by these twisting terrors is Tornado Alley, a path that runs from north-central Texas through central Oklahoma, Kansas, Nebraska, and into the Dakotas. When only the most damaging tornadoes are charted, central Oklahoma is the nation's leading danger zone.

WHAT WAY DO TORNADOES SPIN?

In the northern hemisphere, almost all tornadoes spin counterclockwise, like the water swirling down a bathtub drain. Inside, the tornado acts as a vacuum cleaner, sucking up any and all loose material it encounters.

The relatively rare tornadoes observed to rotate clockwise have been paired with other tornadoes spinning counterclockwise.

THE LIFE OF A TORNADO: SHORT AND VIOLENT

Most tornadoes begin as a "dimple" bulging from the flat wall cloud at the base of a cumulonimbus clouds. This dimple becomes a rotating column of air, or funnel cloud, that descends.

The area punished most by these twisting terrors is Tornado Alley, a path that runs from north-central Texas through central Oklahoma, Kansas, Nebraska, and into the Dakotas

A killer tornado stalks Tracy, Minnesota, June 13, 1968.

When it touches, the funnel cloud is considered a mature tornado, but it doesn't have much time to enjoy being a grown-up—its average life span is less than 15 minutes. At this point the funnel is almost always vertical, reaching its greatest width and its highest potential for destruction. It touches the ground most of the time while it moves, but it does skip or hop from time to time.

Within seven to 10 minutes, on the average, the tornado begins to shrink and it tilts away from the vertical. Then it stretches into a rope shape and often becomes contorted in bizarre forms. Sometimes the end of the funnel flips upward and reattaches itself to the thundercloud above. When it disappears a minute or two later, a tremendous shower of dust and debris carried by the tornado falls to the ground.

An exception to this pattern is some weaker tornadoes formed under conditions that produce air mass thunderstorms. Strong upcurrents can set air whirling on the ground, eventually producing a funnel cloud that rises toward the cloud. Once again, these tornadoes are short-lived.

The average life span of a tornado is less than 15 minutes.

WHAT'S THE DIFFERENCE BETWEEN A TORNADO AND A WATERSPOUT?

A waterspout is a tornado that forms over water, sucking up liquid instead of dust and debris. Some form from supercell thunderstorm clouds, just like tornadoes on land. Others develop in very moist, unstable air in tropical or subtropical areas with a water temperature of 80 degrees Fahrenheit or more. Spinning air near the surface is drawn toward forming clouds by strong updrafts, until it forms a funnel from water to cloud. A relatively few waterspouts form when a tornado passes over water, while a very rare waterspout moves on land to become a tornado.

Most waterspouts form in the summer months in warm waters from the Gulf of Mexico north to about Cape Hatteras, North Carolina. More are spotted in the waters around the Florida Keys than any other area, but meteorologists assume greater numbers are formed in the vastness of unobserved waters.

Waterspouts can cause damage to shipping and coastal facilities. However, because they tend to be short-lived and because they are observable from great distances on water, most vessels avoid them easily, and the annual destruction they cause is limited.

WHAT ARE THE LESSER WHIRLS?

No, they're not an island group in the Indian Ocean or second-class social events. "Lesser whirls" is the fancy name for rotating air pockets that don't quite make it to the big leagues by becoming tornadoes. There are three basic types of lesser whirls.

- *Dust devils* are rapidly rotating columns of air that pick up quantities of dust and other debris. They form primarily over desert areas of the Southwest, where the air doesn't carry sufficient moisture to develop the thunderclouds that form real tornadoes.

- *Snow devils,* the dust devils' cousins, occur most often in high mountain areas.

- *Steam devils* arise from instability produced when there is a great temperature contrast between cold air and warm water. Many form over the geyser-heated waters of Yellowstone National Park.

HOW FAST DOES A TORNADO MOVE?

The average tornado moves along at about 35 miles per hour, so it covers about nine miles before it dies. Some tornadoes have been clocked at 60 to 65 miles per hour (sorry, Officer, I was just trying to keep ahead of that tornado), while others barely move at all. One South Dakota tornado was observed hovering in a field for 45 minutes.

About seven out of every eight tornadoes move in a southwest-to-northeast direction. However, tornadoes have been reported to move in every direction and in patterns such as loops, circles, and zigzags.

HOW LONG AND WIDE IS A TORNADO'S PATH?

Although the average tornado covers about nine miles, the all-time distance record is 293 miles, set by a cyclonic endurance champ on May 26, 1917. This same tornado lasted seven hours and 20 minutes, also an all-time record. Over a 45-year period, only nine tornadoes were found to have traveled 200 miles or more.

A study of 20,000 tornadoes found an average width of 140.8 yards. About half of all tornadoes have widths of 100 yards or less, and only one in 50 was wider than 700 yards.

HOW STRONG ARE TORNADO WINDS?

No wind-measuring instrument has ever survived direct contact with a tornado. So we estimate the speed by a variety of techniques that include tracking particles caught up in the tornado with radar and estimating the force necessary to produce the damage caused by a tornado. Estimated wind speeds range from a low of 50 miles per hour to a high of over 300 miles an hour—an incredible figure.

RATING THE POWER OF TORNADOES

Meteorologists use a system known as the Fujita-Pearson Tornado Intensity Scale to rate tornadoes.

Scale	Category	Force (mph)	Path Length (miles)	Path Width (yd/miles)	Expected Damage
F0	Weak	0–72	0–1	0–17 yds.	Light
F1	Weak	73–112	1–3.1	18–55 yds.	Moderate
F2	Strong	113–157	3.2–9.9	56–175 yds.	Considerable
F3	Strong	158–206	10–31	76–556 yds.	Severe
F4	Violent	207–260	32–99	34–.9 mi.	Devastating
F5	Violent	260–308	100–315	1–3.1 mi.	Incredible

A survey of 20,000 tornadoes that occurred in the U.S. between 1957 and 1977 revealed that 61.6 percent were weak, 36 percent were strong, and only 2.3 percent were violent. But those violent storms caused 68 percent of all tornado damage.

HOW MANY TORNADOES STRIKE THE U.S. EVERY YEAR?

The average is 800 to 900 tornadoes, with the all-time record of 1,115 recorded in 1990. The peak month is May, with an average of 150 tornadoes. Half of all tornadoes strike between April 28 and July 20, a span of just 48 days.

HOW MANY PEOPLE ARE KILLED BY TORNADOES?

In the last century, 15,000 to 20,000 people have suffered tornado-related deaths. Because of more sophisticated warning systems, the current average is about 60 fatalities per year. However, tornado-related damage has increased to an annual average of $1 billion.

CAN TORNADOES BE FORECAST?

The only definitive way to predict when and where a tornado is going to move is to actually observe that tornado. Although meteorologists have become quite sophisticated in detecting the development of clouds that are capable of spawning tornadoes, they have no way of telling which will produce dangerous funnel clouds until those funnel clouds are actually spotted.

However, using sophisticated radar and Skywarn, a vast network of trained weather observers in tornado-prone areas, the National Severe Storms Forecast Center, a division of the National Weather Service, has become much more efficient at detecting tornadoes when they arise and broadcasting warnings over local media.

Meteorologists have no way of telling which storms will produce dangerous funnel clouds.

TORNADO SAFETY PROCEDURES

If your local weather forecast indicates a chance of severe thunderstorms for the day, you should stay tuned to a local radio or television station.

A tornado *watch* means that the weather conditions during a certain period are conducive to the formation of tornadoes. Tornado watches can cover thousands of square miles. You should listen constantly for further weather information, prepare to take shelter, and watch outside for dangerous weather that might be developing.

A tornado *warning* means that one or more tornadoes have been spotted in your area. You should take precautions.

• If possible, take shelter in a tornado cellar or other special excavation. If you don't have a special shelter, go to the basement and stay in the southwest corner. If possible, use furniture to protect yourself and your family—most tornado injuries and deaths are caused by flying debris. If you don't have a basement, stay in a windowless room in the center of the house, such as a closet. If you have time, turn off the main gas and electric service.

• If you are outside, get inside if possible—any structure is better shelter than being out in the open. If you are unable to get inside, run or drive at right angles to the tornado's path. If there is no time to escape, lie flat in the nearest depression or ditch. Do not stay in your vehicle.

• If you have a battery-operated radio, listen constantly and stay where you are until the warning has been lifted.

NATURE'S ONE-EYED MONSTERS: HURRICANES

11

No human being, after looking at a few pictures of Homestead, Florida, after Hurricane Andrew passed through, could have any doubt about what type of weather event deserves the title "greatest storm on Earth." Just 1 percent of the energy in one average hurricane could meet the entire energy needs of the United States for a full year. The force of the winds near the eye of a hurricane is equivalent to an atomic bomb exploding every 10 seconds.

Unlike thunderstorms and tornadoes, which are random and brief weather events, hurricanes form slowly and have a lifespan of a week or more. As we watch satellite photos of the movement of these lumbering one-eyed giants, it seems natural that we call them by name. Some of these names, like those of the madmen and murderers of history, still stick in our memories—Camille, Hugo, Gloria, Bob, and now, Andrew.

I have personally stood in the teeth of hurricane winds. In 1988, Hurricane Gilbert smashed into Mexico, causing terrible destruction. As it moved back into the Gulf of Mexico and headed for Texas, I was assigned to fly to Galveston to do a live remote.

Immediately, some ominous history came to mind. In 1900, a ferocious hurricane struck this low-lying coastal city without warning. The entire city was leveled and an estimated 6,000 people died, the largest death toll inflicted by any hurricane. In 1915, another hurricane killed 275 people in Galveston, the ninth-deadliest storm.

Winds were gentle when I arose in the predawn hours to begin doing my live reports. But in three and a half hours, gusts reached 65 miles per hour, accompanied by driving rain. I literally had to hold onto a utility pole to avoid being blown off my feet, and even though I was shouting, the roar of the winds nearly drowned out my voice. At 9:00 A.M., we quickly packed our gear and raced across the causeway connecting Galveston to the mainland just before it was closed. Fortunately, Gilbert veered at the last moment and spared Galveston the worst of its fury.

Unlike thunderstorms and tornadoes, which are random and brief weather events, hurricanes form slowly and have a lifespan of a week or more.

Unfortunately, Hurricane Hugo didn't spare South Carolina. Once again, I was sent on location—this time to Savannah, Georgia, which was projected to be the target of the storm. This time we were closer to the eye as we broadcast, and the combination of wind, rain, and pounding surf was truly terrifying. After I finished my last live remote for "Good Morning America," I received word that the storm appeared to be heading farther north. My assignment was to hop into a rental car and stay far enough ahead of the storm that I could set up and broadcast. Because hurricane winds rotate counterclockwise, the strongest are located south and west of the eye, the weakest north and east. My technical supervisor and I drove north in gale-force winds, stopping every half hour or so to telephone New York for updates on Hugo's location. We finally settled in Wilmington, North Carolina—just far enough to escape the horrors that were visited upon Charleston, South Carolina.

These encounters with hurricanes gave me a new respect for these immense forces of nature, as well a renewed interest in how hurricanes are formed and the factors that determine their movements.

WHAT IS A HURRICANE?

A hurricane is the most severe form of tropical cyclone, which features counterclockwise movement of air around a low-pressure

A satellite photograph of Hurricane Andrew.

The devastation caused by Hurricane Andrew.

center, that forms in tropical waters. A tropical cyclone with sustained winds of 38 miles per hour or less is called a "tropical depression"; one with sustained winds of 39 to 73 miles per hour is a "tropical storm"; when the winds reach 74 miles an hour or more, the cyclone becomes a "hurricane."

The word hurricane comes from a related group of Central American Indian words that mean "god of stormy weather." A Spanish explorer, Captain Fernando de Oviedo, gave the storm its name when he wrote, "So when the devil wishes to terrify them, he promises them the 'Huracan,' which means 'tempest.'"

WHAT'S THE DIFFERENCE BETWEEN A HURRICANE AND A TYPHOON?

Semantics is the only difference. We use *hurricane* to describe tropical cyclones that form in the western Atlantic Ocean and in the eastern Pacific Ocean off the coasts of Central America and Mexico. These storms account for about one-quarter of all the tropical cyclones that form around the globe each year. These same storms are called *typhoons* in the North Pacific, *cyclones* in the Indian Ocean, *baquiros* in the Philippines, and *willy-willies* in the Timor Sea and northwest Australia.

WHY ARE HURRICANES NAMED?

In 1941, a novelist named George R. Stewart, in a book called *Storm*, created the character of a U.S. Weather Bureau meteorologist who developed the habit of applying women's names to storms as he tracked them across the country. During World War II, naming storms for women became a common practice among Air Force

We use *hurricane* to describe tropical cyclones that form in the western Atlantic Ocean and in the eastern Pacific Ocean off the coasts of Central America and Mexico.

and Navy meteorologists. In 1950, the practice of applying women's names to tropical storms and hurricanes became official. The names were selected by meteorologists from the Weather Bureau and the Armed Services at their annual Hurricane Coordination Conference.

In 1979, men's names made the list for the first time. Today, the names on the annual lists for Atlantic storms are selected by the World Meteorological Organization Region 4 Hurricane Committee from names submitted by the countries affected by these storms.

Names chosen for the next 5 years are:

1993	1994	1995	1996	1997
Arlene	Alberto	Allison	Arthur	Ana
Bret	Beryl	Barry	Bertha	N/A
Cindy	Chris	Chantal	Cesar	Claudette
Dennis	Debby	Dean	Diana	Danny
Emily	Emesto	Erin	Edouard	Erika
Floyd	Florence	Felix	Fran	Fabian
Gert	Gordon	Gabrielle	Gustav	Grace
Harvey	Helene	Humberto	Hortense	Henry
Irene	Isaac	Iris	Isidore	Isabel
Jose	Joyce	Jerry	Josephine	Juan
Katrina	Keith	Karen	Klaus	Kata
Lenny	Leslie	Luis	Lili	Larry
Maria	Michael	Marilyn	Marco	Mindy
Nate	Nadine	Noel	Nana	Nicholas
Ophelia	Oscar	Opal	Omar	Odetta
Phillippe	Patty	Pablo	Paloma	Peter
Rita	Rafael	Roxanne	Rene	Rose
Stan	Sandy	Sebastian	Sally	Sam
Tammy	Tony	Tanya	Teddy	Teresa
Vince	Valerie	Van	Vicky	Victor
Wilma	William	Wendy	Wilfred	Wanda

WHERE DO HURRICANES FORM?

Hurricanes are tropical storms because they need very warm water—at least 80 degrees Fahrenheit—to form. Water north of about 30 degrees latitude is normally too cool.

The area near the equator (0 to 10 degrees north) is also hostile to hurricane formation, because the air currents are almost exclusively vertical; little or no wind can blow.

WHERE DO ATLANTIC HURRICANES FORM?

Atlantic hurricanes form over ocean waters between latitudes 10 degrees north and 30 degrees north. This band has as its southern border a line running across the northern tip of South America to the African coast just below the Cape Verde Islands, and as its northern border a line running through northern Florida, continuing just south of Bermuda, and ending at the African coast south of the Canary Islands.

WHY DO WE HEAR SO MUCH MORE ABOUT ATLANTIC HURRICANES?

The trade winds, the prevailing winds in the latitudes in which hurricanes form, blow from east to west. These prevailing winds, along with the ocean currents and the Azores-Bermuda high, steer many Atlantic hurricanes toward the United States mainland. These same prevailing winds and ocean currents steer most Pacific hurricanes westward, where they die in the middle of the ocean.

WHEN IS THE ATLANTIC HURRICANE SEASON?

Sailors who plied the waters of the Caribbean used to remind themselves about hurricane season with the following rhyme:

June:	Too soon
July:	Stand by
August:	You must
September:	Remember
October:	All over

This poem is an easy way to remember that August and September are the peak months for the most violent hurricanes. Over the period 1886–1990, the Atlantic produced 519 hurricanes (or an average of about five per year). Sixty-six percent of these formed in August and September, while another 18 percent were born in October.

The hurricane season officially begins June 1, but the storms that develop in June and July are normally weak and small. Strong storms can form in the first two weeks of October, but after that the likelihood of a major hurricane drops dramatically until the official end of the season on November 30.

WHAT DOES THE WEATHER IN SENEGAL HAVE TO DO WITH ATLANTIC HURRICANES?

The seeds of Atlantic hurricanes are low-pressure systems moving eastward from West Africa. The climate in West Africa seems to have a direct relationship with the formation of hurricanes— many more hurricanes develop during periods when West Africa has more precipitation than average, while many fewer develop when drought afflicts that area.

Strong storms can form in the first two weeks of October, but after that the likelihood of a major hurricane drops dramatically until the official end of the season on November 30.

DO ALL AFRICAN LOW-PRESSURE SYSTEMS DEVELOP INTO TROPICAL STORMS?

On the contrary, fewer than one in 10 becomes a cyclone. Over one six-year period, just 50 of 609 low-pressure systems moving off the African coast developed into tropical depressions.

For this development to begin, these traveling disturbances from Africa must combine with a complex mix of wind and temperature patterns. When they do, the extremely moist air above the warm waters is pulled upward by a convection current that is strengthened by the tremendous latent heat energy released when water vapor condenses into clouds. This upward pull of air creates a deep low-pressure area at the surface. The Coriolis effect causes the winds sucked into this low-pressure system to begin to swirl. The stronger the convection current and the deeper the low pressure at the center of the storm, the tighter the swirl and the stronger the winds.

WHERE AND WHEN DO PACIFIC HURRICANES FORM?

Pacific hurricanes are born in a more narrow band of waters ranging from 12 degrees to 25 degrees north that extends from the coast of Central America and Mexico to the Pacific south of the Hawaiian Islands. An average of 21 tropical depressions form in this area each year, about twice the number that form in the Atlantic. The season also runs from June to November, with storms equally likely to be spawned any time during this period. On the average, the hurricanes that develop from these tropical depressions are smaller and less powerful than the less frequent Atlantic hurricanes.

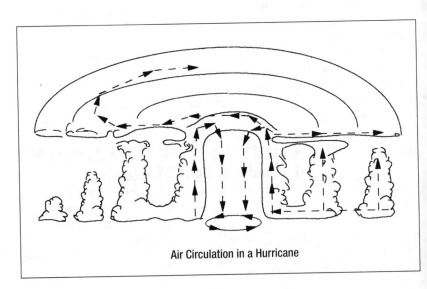

Air Circulation in a Hurricane

WHAT IS THE STRUCTURE OF A HURRICANE?

Hurricanes are giant whirlpools, with an average diameter of 200 to 600 miles. Because their winds spin so fast, they are "tighter" storms than extratropical cyclones, low-pressure systems that form outside the tropics. Also because of this fast spin, they don't form fronts like other low-pressure systems.

The clouds extend to an altitude of 40,000 to 50,000 feet, near the top of the troposphere. The clouds at the top spread out in a flat anvil shape, like a gigantic thundercloud. The spin produces high cirrus clouds that serve as warning of the approaching tempest.

Although the flat anvil cloud at the top makes hurricanes look like a solid cloud mass in satellite photographs, they really consist of bands of intense thunderstorms. A hurricane doesn't bring steady rain, but alternating periods of torrential rain and wind followed by lighter rain and less powerful wind.

The most intense band of wind and rain is the "eye wall," the band closest to the center of the storm. In the strongest hurricanes, such as Hurricane Andrew, this band spins with winds so strong (more than 160 miles per hour) that it is more like a gigantic tornado. These winds are most intense at the surface as they grab moist air and whirl it upward to condense and provide more energy to power the storm. This band, which can be 20 to 30 miles thick, produces by far the most destruction.

At the very center of this devastation, is a strange area called the hurricane's "eye."

WHAT IS THE EYE OF THE HURRICANE?

If you've ever been in the direct path of a hurricane, you've had this strange experience: The storm intensifies for hours until torrential rains and hundred-mile-per-hour winds lash and tear at everything around you. Suddenly, the rain stops, the winds become calm, and the sun comes out. For a few minutes, it seems like the storm has moved far away. Then, in an instant, the calm is replaced by more torrential rain and winds howling from the opposite direction.

This eye of the hurricane, which can be seen very distinctly in satellite photographs, is a calm, circular area in the very center of a hurricane that ranges from seven to 20 miles in diameter. The cause is air that sinks at the very center of the storm, warming and drying as it descends. The eye has the lowest air pressure, the warmest temperatures, and the lowest relative humidity in the storm.

WHAT IS A HURRICANE STORM SURGE?

The intense winds that draw air to the center of a hurricane also draw immense volumes of water. In mid-ocean, where the water is more than 200 feet deep, this water spirals downward, then is carried away by deep ocean currents. As a result, waves at the surface are often as low as three feet.

In shallow water, however, there is no place for this mound of water to go but up. It's driven toward shore along with the hurricane, ever rising until it reaches a peak. When this water crashes on shore at heights that reach 12 to 20 feet, it can cause far more death and destruction in low-lying areas than the force of the hurricane's winds. It was the storm surge in the 1900 hurricane that killed those 6,000 people in Galveston, Texas.

The most dangerous conditions for coastal areas occur when the landfall of the hurricane is at high tide. Because the hurricane's winds blow counterclockwise, the highest surge comes where the winds are blowing directly on shore south and east of the hurricane's eye.

The most dangerous conditions for coastal areas occur when the landfall of the hurricane is at high tide.

WHAT DETERMINES THE PATH OF AN ATLANTIC HURRICANE?

The prevailing trade winds start hurricanes off in a westerly direction. When they get to about 30 degrees north latitude, the mid-latitude westerlies take over, steering the hurricane in a northeast direction.

This general course is often modified to a great degree by the size and position of the Azore-Bermuda High, which spins in a clockwise direction in the middle of the Atlantic Ocean. As powerful as hurricanes are, they cannot penetrate this huge anti-cyclone. If the Azore-Bermuda High is relatively small, its rotation tends to steer hurricanes north, then northeast, away from the United States mainland. If it's large, those winds propel hurricanes in a northwest direction toward the Gulf of Mexico and the southern United States coast. If a trough in the jet stream dips south, disrupting the high, a hurricane may move through the trough to threaten the mid-Atlantic and New England states.

These general rules are little help predicting the course of a specific hurricane if the winds steering it are weak. In this case, hurricanes often seem to careen randomly like a top spinning in a box. They can even form loops upon loops, making forecasters' jobs a nightmare.

HOW DO PACIFIC HURRICANES MOVE?

The typical storm track for Pacific hurricanes takes them north or northwest into an area little traveled by commercial shipping. Occasionally, a hurricane or tropical storm will turn north or northeast. The west coast of Mexico has been struck by hurricane-force storms. However, those that turn further north in the ocean are seriously weakened by the cold (68 degrees Fahrenheit) currents off the United States' western coast, and only in extremely rare cases do they reach the coast as tropical storms.

The terrible destruction caused on the Hawaiian island of Kauai by Hurricane Iniki is also rare: Just six hurricanes threatened Hawaii between 1950 and 1992.

HOW FAST DO HURRICANES MOVE?

In tropical waters, hurricanes lumber along at an average speed of 12 to 16 miles per hour. The slower the speed of the storm, the more devastating the effects of the winds.

However, when hurricanes move far enough to be steered by the much more powerful mid-latitude winds, their speed can accelerate to 25 to 50 miles per hour. This speed dramatically shortens the warning time available for evacuation at points north of Cape Hatteras.

HOW DO WE RATE THE STRENGTH OF HURRICANES?

A scale for placing hurricanes in one of five categories was developed in the early 1970s by Robert Simpson, director of the National Hurricane Center, and Herbert Saffir, a consulting engineer. Here is the Saffir-Simpson Hurricane Damage Potential Scale:

	CATEGORY				
	1	2	3	4	5
Barometric pressure	28.94+	28.5-28.91	27.91-28.47	27.17-27.88	-27.17
Wind speeds (mph)	74-95	95-110	111-130	131-155	156+
Storm surge (feet)	4-5	6-8	9-12	13-18	19+
Damage	Minimal	Moderate	Extensive	Extreme	Catastrophic

In tropical waters, hurricanes lumber along at an average speed of 12 to 16 miles per hour. The slower the speed of the storm, the more devastating the effects of the winds.

HOW STRONG WAS HURRICANE ANDREW?

When Hurricane Andrew arrived near the tip of the Florida peninsula, it was the third-strongest hurricane of the 20th century. A Category 4 storm, it had sustained winds of 145 miles per hour with gusts to 175 miles per hour. Its storm surge was 16.9 feet, an all-time Florida record. The air pressure reading when it came on shore was 27.27 inches of mercury—only Hurricane Camille, which ravaged Mississippi in 1969, and an unnamed hurricane that killed 600 in the Florida Keys in 1935 had lower recorded pressures.

Despite the devastation it caused, Hurricane Andrew's death toll was surpassed by dozens and dozens of hurricanes. The primary reason was the National Hurricane Center's ability to track this relatively slow-moving storm and issue warnings in time for large-scale evacuations.

HOW DOES THE NATIONAL HURRICANE CENTER TRACK HURRICANES?

The National Hurricane Center in Coral Gables, Florida (itself a victim of Hurricane Andrew), tracks storms from the moment of their birth far off in the Atlantic by means of satellite photography and use of sophisticated radar. When the low-pressure system intensifies, the Center sends into the storm one of two WP-3 aircraft operated by the National Oceanic and Atmospheric Administration. This aircraft continues to fly into the storm as it reaches and surpasses hurricane strength. The information collected is fed into Hurricane Center computers to assist forecasters in projecting likely areas and times of impact so that watches and warnings can be issued.

HOW DO HURRICANES DIE?

Making landfall dooms a hurricane, just as stinging dooms a bee. When a tropical cyclone passes from water to land, the source of its energy is cut off and the system begins to weaken. However, the momentum of the storm can carry it hundreds of miles inland. Hurricanes carry an immense amount of moisture, which can cause extensive flooding as the storm slowly deteriorates to a tropical storm, a tropical depression, then just another low-pressure storm system.

Hurricanes also weaken as they pass from tropical to temperate waters in which the temperature drops substantially below 80 degrees Fahrenheit. This is why hurricanes never reach Europe.

A hurricane can regain its strength if it returns to water after a short passage over land, just as Hurricane Andrew did when it reached the Gulf of Mexico after crossing Florida. A few hurricanes from both the Atlantic and the Pacific have crossed Central America and have regained their strength on the other side.

HURRICANE SAFETY PROCEDURES

The approach of any hurricane should be taken very seriously. Because high winds, heavy rains, flooding, and even tornadoes can

Making landfall dooms a hurricane, just as stinging dooms a bee.

cause significant damage more than 100 miles from the center of the storm, you should begin to prepare when a hurricane watch is first issued. These preparations should include stocking nonperishable food, water, emergency lighting, firewood, batteries for portable radios and TVs, and other supplies that will be needed in the event utility service is disrupted for days. You should close storm shutters or board up windows, secure any loose objects or equipment, and make sure all pets are indoors. Finally, you should constantly monitor radio or television broadcasts for further information.

By far the best procedure to follow when a hurricane warning is issued is to evacuate inland. If that is not possible, take refuge in a shelter set up by local governmental officials. Riding out the storm in your home in the face of warnings is not brave, but foolhardy.

By far the best procedure to follow when a hurricane warning is issued is to evacuate inland.

WHAT EXACTLY IS A WEATHERPERSON?

12

One Wednesday in January 1978, I was in the newsroom of WABC in New York (I was doing the weather on the 6 o'clock and 11 o'clock newscasts) when it became apparent that a severe winter snowstorm was poised to strike the Tri-State area. Station management decided to preempt regularly scheduled programming for news coverage that would begin at 3:00 P.M. and continue throughout the night. As part of that coverage, I was dispatched in a van with a camera crew for live reports on how the storm was affecting traffic on a major New Jersey highway.

As it turned out, I became a part of the story of what was happening to commuters all over the New York metropolitan area. As our van emerged from the Lincoln Tunnel that runs under the Hudson River, the snow was falling at an incredible rate. We man-

Another day at the "office," trying to sort out for our viewers at home the many complex factors that determine North American weather patterns.

aged to travel just a couple miles on Route 3 before we were forced to pull over to the side of the road. We set up our equipment, and the anchors back in the newsroom, Roger Grimsby and Bill Beutel, began to go to me for live remotes.

As darkness fell, that location had outlived its usefulness. But the van couldn't move. So my assignment was to trudge, on foot, for two miles to J.P.'s Cafe (in Clifton, N.J.), where another camera crew had sought refuge. By this time, a true blizzard was raging, a rare condition for the metropolitan area. Winds were gusting at 45 to 50 miles per hour, driving the heavy snow horizontally in the subfreezing temperatures. I was well-dressed for bad weather, with boots, gloves, and several layers of clothing. But my face was unprotected. The driving snow felt like thousands of bee stings. Icicles formed on my moustache, and I had to stop every few feet to wipe my glasses. I waded through thigh-deep snow, slipping countless times, during a walk that took me at least an hour.

By the time I stumbled into the cafe, I was nearly frozen and near exhaustion. And, of course, I had to be back on the air in a few minutes. I spent most of the night outside in the blizzard doing reports, then ducking back inside for some Kahlua and coffee to keep my blood circulating. Finally, in the predawn hours, the road crews cleared the highways enough for my crew and me to wind our way home.

My purpose in telling this story isn't to gain your sympathy (although a heartfelt chorus of "poor Spencer" would be much appreciated). Rather, I think it vividly demonstrates how little I understood, at the beginning of my career, what a weatherman's job really entails. As you may recall from my introduction, I had agreed to become a weatherman only because the station manager waved cash in my face. I thought my decision meant that I was abandoning a career as a journalist to become an entertainer.

But, as the story of the blizzard of 1978 demonstrates, I wasn't entertaining anyone out in the driving snow on New Jersey's Route 3. I was reporting a story that affected the lives of millions of viewers as much as any fire, crime, accident, or other event on the news that day. In fact, the areas in which I concentrate much of my reporting—weather and climate—are as important as economics, politics, crime, military affairs, and the other special beats covered by other journalists.

Of course, the weather news isn't always serious, just as a lot of other news isn't always serious—for example, the marital troubles of the British Royal Family. I think I've been successful, in part, because I love to entertain and I love to have fun. But when the weather turns serious, so do I and most of my colleagues who are weather reporters.

WHAT'S THE DIFFERENCE BETWEEN A WEATHER REPORTER AND METEOROLOGIST?

I don't want to dampen your admiration for me or your local weatherperson, but I do want to whet your appetite for the real story behind the forecasts you watch. The truth: Neither the networks nor your local stations create the basic weather forecasts. As I'll describe shortly, analyzing the massive amount of data received from thousands of weather reporting stations, satellites, weather balloons, aircraft, and other sources requires the huge staff and gigantic computing capability of the U.S. Weather Service. All of us rely on the U.S. Weather Service forecasts and computer projections, sometimes in conjunction with additional analysis provided by private weather forecasting services.

That's why I get peeved when some local stations claim that their forecasts are more accurate or useful because the weatherperson on their news is a meteorologist. That's no more true than the claim that a reporter has to be an attorney to cover a trial, an ex-Congressman to cover an election, or an ex-general to cover a war. While I have acquired substantial knowledge of meteorology during my 20 years of reporting the weather, it's my skills as a journalist that enable me to communicate important weather information to you quickly and effectively (and, yes, accurately).

THE PROCESS OF BRINGING WEATHER INFORMATION AND FORECASTS TO YOU

Now that I've climbed down off my high horse, I can saddle you with the real story of how weather information is corralled. Then I'll explain how this information is analyzed and how forecasts are prepared. Finally, I'll explain in detail how I bring you my forecasts every weekday morning on ABC's "World News This Morning" and "Good Morning America."

FROM MAGICIAN TO MAINFRAME: A BRIEF HISTORY OF METEOROLOGY

13

I've often thought that if I could peer 10,000 years back in time, I would see some very distant ancestor of mine rousing himself from sleep before anyone else in the cave, stumbling outside to check conditions, then heading back inside to draw a weather forecast on the cave walls. (No doubt he called it the "Good Morning, *Homo sapiens* Show.") Because early man was far more vulnerable to the elements than we are, Cave Man Christian probably paid a good deal more attention to the subtleties of cloud formations and wind changes than we do. After a few years of such observations, Cave Man was probably able to give his audience a fairly accurate idea of what the weather would be like over the next few hours while they were mammoth-hunting.

Long-term forecasting, however, relied more on the methods of the shaman than the scientist. Cave Man may have read omens in the behavior of animals or plants. He may have relied on dreams or visions. And he probably performed dances or other rituals to persuade his gods to provide the kind of weather most favorable to his people. Though he may have received admiration and awe for his successful predictions or rituals, his failures were no doubt more numerous.

Civilization evolved a lot over the next 9,600 years, but meteorology, the science that seeks to understand the atmosphere and predict the weather, didn't advance with it. The primary reason was that the instruments available to measure the weather remained the same—man's five senses. People could see cloud formations change, hear the wind intensify, feel the temperature change, even smell rain. But they had no way to accurately measure temperature, air pressure, humidity, and wind speed either on the ground or in the upper atmosphere. Humans had no way to obtain any kind of weather information from other areas so that weather systems could be identified and tracked. And even if instruments existed to record weather conditions in a wide variety of areas, people had no way to process and analyze that vast amount of data rapidly enough to produce a forecast.

So the story of meteorology is really the story of the last 400 years, with most of the real advances coming in the last 40.

MEASURING TEMPERATURE

Galileo, who lived from 1564 to 1642, was passionately interested in the study of air. He recognized that air expanded when it was heated, and in 1592, he decided to use that fact to construct a thermometer. This instrument consisted of a large glass bulb filled with air on top of a glass tube resting in a dish of water. When the air was heated, it forced down the level of the water in the glass tube. Measurements of the water level provided the first practical comparative temperature readings.

Over the next decade, Galileo found that this air thermometer was fragile and hard to transport. So he decided to build another instrument based on the fact that liquids also expand when heated. In 1612, he enclosed alcohol in a round bulb connected to a sealed glass tube and found that the level of the alcohol rose and fell with the temperature. Thus Galileo invented the modern thermometer, many of which are still filled with colored alcohol. (Mercury was first used in 1709 by Gabriel Daniel Fahrenheit—more about him shortly.)

However, as significant as the discovery of the thermometer was, a major problem still remained—developing a practical scale of measurement so that temperatures could be accurately compared.

If this is a little confusing, imagine trying to measure the length of your living room without a yardstick or tape measure. You could use the length of your foot, the length of your stride, even the length of your cat's tail. But whatever measurement you came up with wouldn't mean a thing to someone else measuring their living room with a different size foot, a different length stride, or a different cat.

For a hundred years, scientists experimented with scales based on everything from the temperature of melted butter to the temperatures of the blood of various animals. Finally, in 1714, Gabriel Daniel Fahrenheit, a German physicist living in Holland, devised the first scale that became widely used.

WHAT IS THE FAHRENHEIT SCALE?

Because the Fahrenheit scale is one you and I still use every day, we'd like to think that its inventor based it on some clever and consistent scientific measurements. The truth: Fahrenheit picked as "0" the point to which the mercury sank on a particularly cold day in Danzig. For some reason, he assigned the number 96 to his

*F*or a hundred years, scientists experimented with scales based on everything from the temperature of melted butter to the temperatures of the blood of various animals.

erroneous measurement of the average temperature of the human body. The interval between these points was divided into 96 equal divisions, or degrees. Using this illogical scale, the freezing point of water fell at 32 degrees and the boiling point of water was 212 degrees. Even though Fahrenheit's scheme made little more practical sense than those based on the blood temperature of a goat, people were evidently so eager to have any kind of scale that it caught on.

WHAT IS THE CENTIGRADE TEMPERATURE SCALE?

A Swedish astronomer named Anders Celsius developed a more logically based scale in 1742. He assigned "0" to the reading at the freezing point of water and "100" to the reading at the boiling point of water. The Celsius, or Centigrade, scale, a division into 100 equal degrees (or 100 centigrades), is widely used in scientific circles as well as in most countries.

WHAT IS THE KELVIN TEMPERATURE SCALE?

The most exacting scale for scientific measurement was developed by Lord Kelvin, an English scientist, in 1850. Kelvin used as 0 the absolute lowest point at which temperature can exist, a point at which all molecular motion stops completely. This "absolute zero" is -459.72 degrees Fahrenheit and -273.18 degrees Celsius. Water freezes at 273 degrees Kelvin and boils at 373 degrees Kelvin. The Kelvin Scale is used primarily by scientists.

HOW DO YOU CONVERT FAHRENHEIT TO CENTIGRADE, AND VICE-VERSA?

Meteorologists seem to love complicated formulas, but most of us weatherpeople wish that Fahrenheit and Celsius had sat down together, had a couple of beverages, and worked out their differences. Since they didn't, we're stuck with the following:

- To convert Centigrade into Fahrenheit:

  F = 9/5C + 32.

If it's 30 degrees Centigrade, you multiply 30 times 9/5 to get 54, then add 32 to arrive at a Fahrenheit temperature of 86.

- To convert Fahrenheit into Centigrade:

  C = 5/9 (F-32)

If it's 72 degrees Fahrenheit, you subtract 32 from 72 to get 40,

The Celsius, or Centigrade, scale, a division into 100 equal degrees (or 100 centigrades), is widely used in scientific circles as well as in most countries.

then multiply by 5/9 to arrive at about 22 degrees Centigrade.

Unless you've got a fraction fixation, you might want to memorize Spencer's Simple Centigrade System. First, remember that 0 degrees Centigrade equals 32 degrees Fahrenheit. Then remember:

Below zero Centigrade: It's cold! Below freezing
1–10 degrees C.: It's chilly—32 to 50 degrees F.
10–20 degrees C.: Spring and fall weather, 51–68 degrees F.
20–30 degrees C.: Summertime, 69–86 degrees F.

WHAT'S THE DIFFERENCE BETWEEN ALCOHOL AND MERCURY THERMOMETERS?

Mercury is more accurate than alcohol, so it's used in most thermometers that measure small differences such as body temperature. But mercury freezes at about -30 degrees Fahrenheit and it's more expensive, so alcohol is used in most home air thermometers.

WHEN WERE THE OTHER MAJOR WEATHER INSTRUMENTS INVENTED?

I've already explained how Galileo's assistant, Evangilista Torricelli, invented the mercury barometer in 1643. The other major instruments were invented in:

1667 Anemometer (wind speed)
1773 Hair hygrometer (humidity)
1825 Psychrometer (dew point)

WHEN WERE THESE INSTRUMENTS FIRST USED TO CREATE FORMAL WEATHER RECORDS?

The leading patron of European studies in the time of Galileo was the Grand Duke of Tuscany. Shortly after the invention of the thermometer and the barometer, he began keeping accurate records and he tried to establish a system of weather recording stations in northern Italy. The system soon fell apart, but the practice of keeping records spread to other European cities.

The first instrument weather readings in the United States were recorded by John Lining in Charleston, South Carolina, beginning in 1738. Other systemic efforts were begun in New Haven, Connecticut, in 1780, Baltimore in 1817, and Philadelphia in 1825. Then, over the next two decades, the Medical Department of the U.S. Army instructed many of its military posts to begin taking and recording daily weather instrument readings.

Over a period of time, these records provided a detailed portrait of the climate in a certain location. In 1820, Heinrich Brandes, a

> Mercury is more accurate than alcohol, so it's used in most thermometers that measure small differences such as body temperature.

German scientist, came up with the important idea that weather could best be studied by creating a map of weather conditions across a large area at the same time. Brandes eventually produced the world's first weather map—containing weather data that was exactly 37 years old. (I hear he sold one copy—to Rip Van Winkle.) Obviously, without a way to collect information more quickly, forecasting the movement of weather systems was impossible.

SAMUEL MORSE SAVES THE DAY: THE IMPORTANCE OF THE TELEGRAPH

In 1844, Samuel F. B. Morse clicked the following message, which was transported instantly by wire from Baltimore to Washington: "What hath God wrought?" Almost immediately, scientists in the United States and Europe realized that what He had wrought was a great way to collect weather information quickly. Just five years later, in 1849, under the auspices of the Smithsonian Institution, Americans Joseph Henry and James Espy gathered the first telegraphic weather reports, which consisted of one-word descriptions (*e.g.*, "clear," "rain," "cloudy") sent in by telegraph operators. Shortly afterward, the first weather service was established under the direction of the War Department.

The first weather map published on the same day that the weather occurred (imagine that!) was made in England on August 8, 1851. The first use of a telegraph system for forecasting severe storms and other major weather events was set up in France in 1854. The first official United States forecast was released on November 9, 1870. (It described a storm system moving across the Great Plains, warned of high winds along the shores of the Great Lakes, and forecast fair weather for the East Coast as a high pressure system moved in.)

HOW ACCURATE WERE THESE EARLY FORECASTS?

The man on the street in 1875 had about the same opinion of weather forecasts as the man on the street in 1993—"not good enough." The 19th-century public didn't appreciate the fact that for the first time in human history, telegraphic reports provided the first warnings of storm systems that were moving over land. The first forecasts were heralded as great scientific advances. The problem was—and is still today—that people associated the word "scientific" with the concept "100-percent accuracy." People expected the forecast weather to arrive with the predictability of the Century Limited train from Chicago. When it didn't, weather forecasters and forecasting came under significant public derision both in the United States and in Europe.

These expectations were way beyond the limited capability of

The first weather map published on the same day that the weather occurred was made in England on August 8, 1851.

the weather services of the time. Although weather stations provided accurate ground reports, forecasters had no knowledge of nor any ability to measure upper-level winds (nobody knew the jet stream even existed). Furthermore, all local reports coming in over the wire had to be logged in, compiled, and analyzed by hand. Forecasters had little time to do anything but spot major systems and guess where they were likely to move.

In the face of public disdain for their prognostications, meteorologists became as disenchanted with the process of forecasting as the general public had with their results—in England, the national weather service gave up forecasting entirely in 1865 for more than two decades. Weather services around the world concentrated more on collecting statistics and describing weather events.

REVOLUTIONARY STEP 2: UP, UP, AND AWAY
IN OUR BEAUTIFUL BALLOONS

The association between weather forecasters and hot air is no doubt a close one in your mind. But *hot air* in meteorology refers to the practice of sending balloons into the upper atmosphere to record weather information and track upper-level winds. Use of these balloons opened up a whole new chapter in the history of meteorology.

Although scientists from the time of Leonardo da Vinci had speculated about the hot air principle of flight, the first balloon, a 105-foot-circumference construction of linen and paper made by the Montgolfier brothers, didn't take flight over Paris until 1783. Later that year, a French physicist came up with the idea of filling a balloon with recently discovered gas called "inflammable air," or hydrogen. As a distinguished crowd watched the balloon rise from the Champs de Mars, one man turned to the American ambassador, Benjamin Franklin, and asked, "Of what use is a balloon?" Franklin replied, "Of what use is a newborn baby?"

As usual, Franklin was an astute judge of scientific potential. Within a decade, men were riding balloons into the upper atmosphere with thermometers and barometers. Others sent balloons up to track upper-level winds. However, gathering detailed information by balloon did not become widespread until about 1892, when the perfection of self-recording weather instruments made it unnecessary for men to go aloft. These balloons were designed to burst at certain altitudes, then fall to Earth with the deflated balloon serving as a parachute.

As balloon studies became a daily routine, meteorologists began to understand that weather is often determined by the movement of large air masses. They also began to appreciate how upper-level winds guide these air masses. They found that data from the upper atmosphere was often more useful in weather forecasting than data collected at ground level.

WORLD WAR I LEADS TO FURTHER UNDERSTANDING

During the Great War, Allied countries stopped broadcasting public weather reports and forecasts so the enemy couldn't hear them. This also cut off the flow of information to neutral countries such as Norway. Forced to rely on their own resources, Norwegian meteorologists intensively studied information gathered from a variety of sources, including balloons, to develop one of the most significant methods of weather study—analyzing air masses and the weather created when they collide. The Norwegians saw the middle latitudes as a battleground between armies of air. They began keeping close track of moving masses of air that differed from one another and noting the positions and movements of their borders (or fronts).

The result was a significant increase in the accuracy of short-term weather forecasting. Between World War I and World War II, using airplanes to gather data as well as balloons, meteorologists increased their knowledge of upper-air movements and, as a result, the accuracy of their forecasts. These new forecasting skills turned out to be a crucial advantage in the air raids that played such a pivotal role in defeating Germany and Japan.

REVOLUTIONARY STEP 3: COMPUTERS

You may be surprised that I don't mention the development of radar and the launching of weather satellites as "revolutionary steps" in forecasting. Although both are extremely important, they are really more sophisticated ways to track the movement of air masses and fronts. What was really revolutionary was the use of balloons that provided the data that led the way to the discovery of the critical role these elements play in our daily weather. As for radar and satellites, I'll describe their use when I explain how the daily forecast for your area is prepared and delivered to you.

The development of computers, however, did lead to a third revolution in weather forecasting. Preparing detailed weather forecasts depends on processing an enormous amount of data from weather stations all over the country, then comparing that data to data collected over the course of many years to analyze what weather patterns are likely to develop in the future. Before computers, such sophisticated analysis was well beyond the practical range of human ability.

In the late 1950s, the U.S. Navy, the U.S. Air Force, and the U.S. Weather Bureau combined to form the Joint Numerical Weather Prediction Unit ("numerical prediction" is the term used to describe the application of high-speed computers to analyzing weather patterns). For almost two decades, the results were

One man turned to the American ambassador, Benjamin Franklin, and asked, "Of what use is a balloon?" Franklin replied, "Of what use is a newborn baby?"

mixed. Numerical forecasting proved helpful in predicting changes in upper-atmosphere patterns, but were of little use in making ground-level local forecasts.

However, in the late 1970s, dramatic increases in computer technology and software led to a dramatic increase in the ability of computers to analyze weather information. Today, the supercomputer at the National Meteorological Center prepares three different weather models twice each day. Preparing the least complicated of these three models without the computer would require a staff of 123,000 people.

WHERE ARE WE TODAY?

Meteorologists today employ a sophisticated network of weather observation stations, high-tech surveillance techniques, and supercomputers in the task of preparing tomorrow's forecast. But the best forecasters still use a dash of the same techniques used 10,000 years ago by primitive shamans (and Cave Man Christians). Keen observation, experience, and old-fashioned intuition often make the difference between average and superior forecasting.

B ut the best forecasters still use a dash of the same techniques employed 10,000 years ago by primitive shamans.

MODERN TECHNOLOGY: RECORDING AND MEASURING THE WEATHER TODAY

14

In the 19th-century, gathering weather information was not a task for the weak or the faint of heart. Obtaining an accurate measurement of the wind speeds, air pressure, and temperature in the upper atmosphere required bundling up in several layers of clothes, climbing into a balloon basket, and ascending to staggering heights. Frostbite was an occupational hazard, and because the air becomes very thin at altitudes above 20,000 feet, these brave men risked death from asphyxiation as they gathered air samples from heights that reached 29,000 feet.

These intrepid aeronauts conducted a wide variety of experiments that included, in one case, sitting on a horse while the balloon ascended. (Note: If you've ever wondered why Mr. Ed was never chosen as an astronaut, you'll be interested to know that horses suffer nosebleeds at relatively low altitudes.) But while they made some important discoveries about the atmosphere, they didn't contribute to increased accuracy of daily weather forecasts. One balloon ascension provided information for only one isolated location at one point in time. To forecast the weather, meteorologists needed the ability to monitor conditions on the ground and aloft with regularity and over vast geographic areas.

The development of instruments that could record conditions in unmanned balloons was an important first step. It led to an impressive system of observation and data collection used by the National Weather Service today. This system includes manned weather stations, unmanned weather stations, aircraft flights, twice-daily balloon launches, radar, and satellites.

THE RAW MATERIAL OF WEATHER FORECASTS

The information collected by the National Weather Service is very basic:

- Temperature

- Air pressure
- Pressure tendency (Is the pressure rising or falling?)
- Wind speed
- Wind direction
- Dew point
- Current weather conditions (clear, overcast, raining, etc.)

What isn't so simple is obtaining these readings from enough locations to produce meaningful forecasts. The rule of thumb in meteorology is that accurate one-day forecasts require detailed information about weather all over North America; three-day forecasts require detailed information about weather over the entire western hemisphere; and five-day forecasts require detailed information about weather over the entire globe. And we're not talking about just ground-level readings—forecasters need information about conditions at altitudes up to a minimum of 10 to 12 miles.

If this sounds like a monumental effort, you're right. Producing meaningful, accurate forecasts requires obtaining frequent information from tens of thousands of sources. Today, these sources are a combination of manned weather stations and a variety of high-tech devices.

WEATHER REPORTING STATIONS

Spencer's Quick Quiz: If you were looking for about a thousand locations where people keenly interested in weather conditions were on duty 24 hours a day, what kind of location do you think you'd find? If you answered, "Airports, of course," you win a hearty "Well done!"

You'll be pleased to know that the National Weather Service came up with the same answer a long time ago. With the cooperation of the Federal Aviation Administration, the Weather Service receives current weather information every hour from almost 1,000 airports across the United States. Every three hours, the Weather Service computers record current weather information from almost 100,000 airports and other locations around the world. Added to this impressive total are reports from ships and aircraft.

The National Weather Service has also been increasing its use of unmanned stations. At sea, automated weather buoys hourly provide important information about the ocean areas in which much of our weather is formed. On land, the Weather Service has been installing automated weather instruments in locations not served by fully manned airports. This Automated Surface Observing System, which will ultimately consist of 1,000 unmanned stations, will fill important gaps in the present reporting system.

W̲ith the cooperation of the Federal Aviation Administration, the Weather Service receives current weather information every hour from almost 1,000 airports across the United States.

Among my favorite assignments are weather duets with local weather experts, such as Larry the Weather Lama, forecaster for our sister network in Lima, Peru.

VOLUNTEER WEATHER OBSERVERS

At about 12,000 locations in the United States, private citizens have volunteered to record daily instrument readings and weather observations. Once a month, these records are sent to the National Weather Service, where they provide valuable information on climate and climate changes.

Most of the National Weather Service's 300 local offices have also trained volunteers to serve as spotters for violent weather, such as tornadoes. This early warning system often saves lives.

BALLOONS

Weather stations, manned and unmanned, provide information only about ground conditions. For a three-dimensional look at the weather, we still rely on that old standby, the weather balloon.

The package that balloons carry today is far more sophisticated than the instruments carried in the past. Called a "radiosonde," this package features a lightweight box that includes instruments measuring air pressure, relative humidity, and temperature. The package also includes a device that allows the balloon to be tracked from the ground (so wind speed and direction can be calculated) and a radio transmitter that constantly sends the collected data to the ground.

Through a cooperative international effort, about 500 balloons are launched worldwide twice a day at the same time—noon and midnight Greenwich Mean Time. That's 7:00 A.M. and 7:00 P.M. Eastern Standard Time, 6:00 A.M. and 6:00 P.M. Central Standard

Through a cooperative international effort, about 500 balloons are launched worldwide twice a day at the same time—noon and midnight Greenwich Mean Time.

Time, etc. The balloons rise for 45 to 90 minutes until they reach an altitude between 90,000 and 120,000 feet. Then the balloons burst and the packages fall back to Earth (one-third to one-half are recovered to be reused).

WEATHER SATELLITES

The launching of the first weather satellite revolutionized weather data collection. For the first time, meteorologists could spot and continuously follow hurricanes and other storm systems that developed in the world's oceans, far from land reporting stations. Today, the National Hurricane Center relies almost exclusively on satellite photographs to track tropical systems and project their future courses.

The National Weather Service collects information and photographs from two different kinds of satellites. The photographs of cloud cover over the United States that you see on TV every day are taken by a satellite in a geostationary orbit. That is, the orbiting speed of these satellites (called GEOS for "Geostationary Operational Environmental Satellite") is identical to that of the Earth's rotation, so the satellite stays "parked" over a specific spot about 22,000 miles above the equator.

From this lofty perch, a GEOS satellite does more than take black-and-white photographs of clouds. It carries instruments that can measure water vapor in the air and the temperatures at the top of clouds and in the upper atmosphere. A GEOS also receives signals from weather buoys, unmanned weather stations, ships and planes, and other sources, signals that are beamed back down to the National Weather Service headquarters in Virginia.

The second type of satellite flies much lower (about 530 miles) in an orbit that takes it over both poles. Because of this lower orbit, these satellites take pictures with a much higher degree of resolution and gather more detailed information about water vapor, cloud formations, and air temperature than does a GEOS satellite. The problem is that a satellite in polar orbit can photograph and scan only an approximately 100-mile-wide swath of the Earth's surface on each pass. That means that each satellite passes over a specific spot only twice each day. The four polar satellites in orbit photograph each location a total of eight times a day, while a GEOS satellite transmits a picture of North America every half hour.

To obtain better data, the National Weather Service is working on advanced GEOS satellites with much more sophisticated and sensitive equipment.

RADAR

We hear about radar (an acronym for "radio detection and rang-

The four polar satellites in orbit photograph each location a total of eight times a day, while a GEOS satellite transmits a picture of North America every half hour.

ing") all the time. But while most of us are familiar with what it does (tracking storms, aircraft, etc.), few of us are actually able to define what it is and how it works. You'll be pleased to know that, in stark contrast to a lot of meteorological gadgets, radar is pretty simple to understand.

The roots of this invention go all the way back to 1888, when a German physicist named Heinrich Hertz proved that metal objects reflect radio waves. It occurred to other physicists that by measuring the time it took for radio waves to bounce off an object and return (radio waves travel at the speed of light), you could find out how far away that object was. But little other than tinkering was done with this idea until the 1930s, when the world was on the brink of war. In the coming conflict, radar was to prove incredibly valuable in locating enemy targets.

Weather radar is based on the fact that moisture in the air will also reflect radio waves. Heavier rain will reflect more of the radio signals than light rain or drizzle. The equipment receiving the return signals records the intensities and distance and converts them to maps that use different colors to show different intensities of precipitation. Radar provides continuous observation of precipitation within 150 to 200 miles of the radar site.

The National Weather Service will soon benefit from the installation of NEXRAD, or Next Generation Radar. This system, funded by the departments of Transportation and Commerce, involves the installation of 100 high-powered radars based on the discovery of an Austrian physicist. Way back in 1842, Christian Doppler discovered that the whistle of a train approaching a location had a higher pitched frequency than the same whistle of a train moving away from a location. This phenomenon is called the Doppler effect. Doppler radar detects the difference between winds blowing toward the radar station and winds blowing away. Most important, it can detect the twisting winds of mesocyclones that spawn tornadoes and downburst, or wind shear, that can cause plane crashes. Doppler radars installed in tornado-prone Oklahoma and in the Washington, D.C., area have proven to be extremely effective in bringing to light otherwise undetectable dangerous weather conditions.

Weather radar is based on the fact that moisture in the air will also reflect radio waves.

WIND PROFILERS

To provide a constant picture of the shifting winds and air masses in the upper atmosphere, the National Weather Service has begun installing a network of devices called "wind profilers." Each profiler has a 40-foot-by-40-foot antenna that looks like a giant metal checkerboard. This device, which is actually called a "phased array antenna," sends radio waves into the atmosphere at various angles. Slight changes in air density reflect waves back to the antenna. Computers can then compute changes of wind speed and direction at 72 different levels, ranging up to 10 to 12 miles.

Eventually, wind profilers will replace the twice-daily balloon launchings. The constant monitoring of upper-atmosphere conditions should lead to more accurate short-term weather forecasts.

PUTTING IT ALL TOGETHER: PREPARING TODAY'S FORECAST

15

Recording weather conditions all over the globe and collecting that data is a gargantuan task, but one that presents primarily logistical problems that are being overcome by technical advances. Eventually, with adequate funding, up-to-date weather conditions from all levels of the atmosphere all over the globe will be available to meteorologists.

However, turning that data into more accurate forecasts, especially long-range forecasts, presents more complicated problems. To get an idea of exactly how difficult the process is, imagine trying to predict the exact flight pattern of a paper airplane launched from the top of a windy hill. Analyzing data about air currents, air pressure, humidity, the terrain, and the design specification of the paper craft, a computer could provide a general profile of the projected flight pattern. But a hundred unpredictable variables—from a slight tear in the plane to the coincidental flight of a bird—could render that projection useless.

The application of technology will increase the accuracy of weather forecasts in the future. But, as we'll see, the element of unpredictability will continue to make weather forecasting one of the most frustrating and challenging of scientific tasks.

THE COMPUTER: WEATHER FORECASTING'S REAL STAR

I hope that all of you watch me every morning to find out what the weather's going to be that day, and I'm sure that you have a favorite local weatherperson who provides information about future weather on your evening news. But both your local weatherperson and I have to admit that the real star of weather forecasting is terribly unphotogenic, never makes appearances at shopping malls and county fairs, and (horrors!) has never uttered a single pun. And who is this pundit? A mass of silicon chips and printed circuits known as Cray YMP-832.

When this supercomputer was put on line about three years ago, it upgraded the National Weather Service's capacity to process information from 200 million calculations per second to 2 billion calculations per second. As I pointed out before, the computer accomplishes what 123,000 people (without taking into consideration coffee breaks, personal phone calls, and daydreaming) would be needed to do.

This star computer (let's name it "Crayg") absorbs the immense volume of data coming into the National Weather Service and turns it into 20,000 forecasts and 6,000 weather maps each day. How Crayg performs this task highlights both the potential for increased accuracy in the future and the practical limits to forecasting.

THE GRID SYSTEM: THE APPROACH TO NUMERICAL PREDICTION

The U.S. Weather Service computer generates 20,000 forecasts and 6,000 weather maps each day.

To understand how the supercomputer goes about predicting the weather, imagine that you're in charge of a horse ranch covering millions of acres of prairie. Your job is to monitor constantly dozens of herds of horses roaming that ranch to spot problems and

Here I am just before air time. "Hello, Dial-a-Forecast?"

predict where the herds are headed. Sending out cowboys at random on horseback, in jeeps, or in airplanes would be a confusing waste of time. What you'd have to do instead is to take a map and divide the ranch into squares, or grids. Then you'd assign one cowboy to monitor that grid. By analyzing the reports from each grid you could put together a picture of where the herds were, in what directions they'd been moving, and what conditions (e.g., predators or water holes) might be affecting what they were running from or moving toward. Your accuracy in locating herds and predicting their movements will depend largely on the size of the grids you establish—a cowboy can cover five square miles more quickly and thoroughly than 50 square miles.

The National Weather Service also uses the grid approach to analyzing weather data and making predictions. But because weather takes place up to the top of the troposphere, its approach has to be three dimensional. The world is divided into about 3,000 grids that cover seven separate levels from the ground to a height of 10 to 12 miles.

THE IMPORTANCE OF MODELS

Crayg, our supercomputer, spends a great deal of the day looking at incredibly complicated models of how the Earth's atmosphere behaves when certain conditions occur. Scientists have constructed these models by applying the laws of advanced mathematics and fluid dynamics to the records of exactly how the atmosphere has behaved over the last few decades. They do this for the same reason that many baseball managers are using computers that can tell them that a certain batter hits curve balls from a right-handed pitcher to the left side of the diamond 14 percent of the time.

Because so many factors combine in determining the weather, the National Weather Service has created a number of different models. The importance assigned each type of weather information is weighted differently in each model. For example, one model may place a heavy emphasis on changes in air pressure, while another is weighted toward changes in upper-level winds.

PUTTING IT ALL TOGETHER

Twice a day, after the information from balloon launches all over the globe is received, the National Weather Service's supercomputer sets about the task of analyzing information from each of the 3,000 grids. Next, taking into consideration the weather from surrounding grids, the computer forecasts how the weather will change in every individual grid in every 10-minute interval over the next 12 hours. Using its various existing models, the computer generates twice-a-day forecasts for 12 hours, 24 hours, and 48 hours after the initial time for each grid. Once a day, the computer extends the forecasts to the next three to 10 days.

The forecasts for each grid are combined to produce forecasts and weather maps for local areas, the entire United States, and the entire globe. This information is then transmitted to local Weather Service offices and private weather forecasters.

IF THIS COMPUTER IS SO TERRIFIC, WHY DO WE NEED LOCAL FORECASTERS?

One of the hardest jobs faced by forecasters is predicting whether precipitation will fall as rain or snow.

Local forecasters—the local offices of the National Weather Service, private weather forecasting companies, and media forecasters—play a vital role for a number of reasons.

First, the forecasts based on the four or five computer models most frequently used may differ considerably. Sometimes one model calls for heavy rain, while another predicts fair weather. In these cases, local forecasters rely on more detailed local records, on their personal experience, and on plain old-fashioned intuition to choose which model has produced the more likely scenario. While certain forecasters are more skilled than others, none are infallible—I've had stunning successes and some spectacular failures.

Second, local weather personnel often specialize in detailed areas of the forecasts. For example, each Weather Service office has a meteorologist in charge of aviation forecasts and marine forecasts. A private forecaster hired by the local transportation department may focus exclusively on predicting the amount of snowfall, while another hired by local utilities concentrates on the likelihood of damaging winds. The use of in-depth knowledge of the subtleties of local weather and the use of specialized local instruments, as well as the assistance of local observers, produce more accurate specific forecasts than the general forecasts issued by the supercomputer.

Third, conditions often change dramatically between the time the computer begins making its calculations and the next forecasting period—winds can change direction, temperatures can rise or fall, storms can even blow in. A forecast of fair weather issued at noon can seem ridiculous when it's pouring during the six-o'clock news.

One of the hardest jobs faced by forecasters is predicting whether precipitation will fall as rain or snow, because a temperature difference of just one or two degrees can make an enormous difference. When I was a weatherman in Baltimore, the rain-snow line commonly ran right through my forecasting area. I would change the position of that line on my weather maps several times in the course of the afternoon as I received updated temperature readings from dozens of locations. My resulting forecast was more accurate than any computer-issued forecast.

WHAT ELSE INFLUENCES
THE ACCURACY OF PREDICTIONS?

Other factors influence the accuracy of local forecasts.

• Range of typical weather. In some parts of our country, you can be a champion forecaster by simply uttering, "The weather tomorrow will be the same as today." (In fact, such a prediction, which meteorologists label a "persistence forecast," is accurate about half the time almost everywhere.) The weather is so consistent in Hawaii that there are no TV weatherpeople and no forecasts on the local news. Weather is similarly consistent in the desert areas over much of the year. On the other hand, weather in the Midwest and along the East Coast often changes dramatically in very short periods.

• Geographic location in the U.S. Forecasts generally become more accurate as we shift our focus from west to east. The reason: Most of our weather moves from west to east, and the National Weather Service is a lot better equipped to track weather moving over the continental United States than it is weather moving over the oceans.

• The seasons: The weather in certain areas can be much more unpredictable in certain seasons of the year. For example, the clash of warm moist air masses and cold Canadian air masses often spawns violent weather over much of the Midwest and the Plains states in the spring.

• Changing global weather patterns. A combination of global weather patterns produced a large area of high pressure that dominated the central United States during the spring and summer of 1988, producing a severe drought. As a result, the weather forecasts for the region varied little from day to day for months, until the global pattern changed again.

SO, SPENCER, AFTER YOU'VE HEDGED YOUR BETS,
HOW ACCURATE ARE FORECASTS, ANYWAY?

The installation of our buddy Crayg and continuing advances in weather reporting have produced significant increases in accuracy over the last 10 years. Here's where we stand today.

• Twelve to 24-hour forecasts. These short-term forecasts are pretty much on the mark about seven out of eight days. The

One of the things I truly enjoy about my job is the opportunity to promote worthwhile causes, such as literacy.

biggest problem is predicting when and where severe local storms, such as the supercell thunderstorms that spawn tornadoes, will arrive.

> *Second-day forecasts today are about as accurate as 24-hour forecasts were 10 years ago.*

- Twenty-four to 48 hours. Thanks to the supercomputer, second-day forecasts today are about as accurate as 24-hour forecasts were 10 years ago. The forecast for general weather conditions are accurate about eight out of 10 days.

- Three to five days. Forecasts can generally predict the movement of large air masses and storms quite well up to five days. Forecasts of daily temperatures are more accurate than forecasts of precipitation. A decade ago, three-day forecasts were accurate about 55 percent of the time; now, five-day forecasts are that accurate, with the percentage of three-day forecasts on the mark increasing to about 65 percent.

- Six to 10 days. Temperature trends are forecast fairly well, with the likelihood of major precipitation being moderately accurate. However, we can't accurately forecast day-to-day weather over such an extended period.

- Thirty- and 90-day forecasts. All we can do is indicate that temperature and precipitation are likely to average above or below normal over these periods. The success rate of these expert projections is, to date, only slightly better than tossing a coin or reading tea leaves. And even though I know you're dying to find out how the weather will be for opening day at the ballpark next spring, I have to tell you that predicting day-to-day weather over such a time span is totally impossible.

WHAT ABOUT THE FORECASTS IN THE OLD FARMER'S ALMANAC?

Before you *Farmer's Almanac* fans get ready to douse me with maple syrup and toss me on an anthill, let me say that I'm a big admirer, too. I think they do a terrific job of detecting the subtle changes in global weather patterns that make it probable that certain areas of the country will have drier summers or snowier winters than average. However, if you can prove that their predictions of a heavy snowfall or other major weather event on a specific day are consistently more accurate than pure chance, I'll take my own sticky bath and plop on that anthill.

WHAT WILL MAKE FORECASTING MORE ACCURATE?

No, the answer's not Spencer Christian's retirement. Shame on you! Instead, increased accuracy will depend on the following changes:

• Better monitoring of ocean weather. 70 percent of the world's weather takes place over the 70 percent of the globe that's covered by water. The only practical way to take readings of the weather conditions in this vast area is by launching a greater number of sophisticated weather satellites. More frequent and accurate data will fill in what are often gaping holes in the information now used to compile long-range forecasts.

• More frequent measurements of the upper atmosphere.Much more accurate information about the high-level winds and movement of storm systems will be available when a system of wind profilers, which provide constant readings, replace the twice-daily balloon launches. More sophisticated satellites will also increase the data available.

• Faster computers. As fond as I am of good old Crayg, I know he's inevitably headed for the junk heap. Installing faster computers that can handle more data is like hiring more cowboys for the ranch—the grids can be smaller. That means more accurate forecasting. Faster computers can also handle more sophisticated atmospheric models.

• Completion of NEXRAD. Short-term forecasting of severe weather will be dramatically improved when the country is completely covered by Doppler radar systems.

In the foreseeable future, meteorologists expect the following improvements:

• Twelve- to 48-hour forecasts: Near 100-percent accuracy with swift detection of tornadoes and other severe local weather.

• Three- to five-day forecasts: Accuracy approaching that of the one- and two-day forecasts today.

• Six- to 10-day forecasts: Reasonably accurate day-by-day predictions.

• Thirty-day forecasts and beyond: Much more accurate predictions about the probability of temperatures and precipitation that are above or below normal levels.

WHY PERFECT FORECASTING IS IMPOSSIBLE

When I discussed fronts and storms earlier in this book, I described the famous dishpan experiment conducted at the University of Chicago. To refresh your memory, scientists rigged up a dishpan that was cooled at the center to represent the pole and heated at the edges to represent the equator. Water was added, and the dishpan was placed on a turntable at a speed equivalent to that of the Earth's rotation. The water formed currents just like the jet stream and whirls and eddies like the highs and lows of the atmosphere.

One other element puzzled researchers—the movement of the currents and the appearance and disappearance of the whirls and eddies seemed to be totally unpredictable. At the time, scientists assumed that they were overlooking some factor that, when discovered, would make the movements of the water (and thus the atmosphere) more predictable.

That assumption was shattered by Edward Lorenz, a meteorologist at the Massachusetts Institute of Technology (MIT). Back in the early 1960s, Lorenz created some sophisticated models that, when programmed into a computer, produced changing patterns that were a lot like the changes in real weather. One day, he decided to check some of his calculations. To save time, he started in the middle rather than at the beginning, and he programmed the numbers to three decimal places (e.g., 5.432) instead of to six decimal places (e.g., 5.432165). To his astonishment, the mathematically insignificant changes produced dramatic changes in the end result.

Lorenz's findings were the first step in the development of what is now called chaos theory, which has had a great effect on many different sciences. In meteorology, it means that no matter how accurate instruments and computer models become, there will be tiny changes in conditions that are too small to monitor. But over a period of time, these conditions will produce such a dramatic difference between projections and reality as to render the forecasts meaningless.

What this means is that as soon as we assure ourselves of forecasts of conditions that allow people adequate time to avoid tornadoes, hurricanes and other severe storms, we should divert money and energy from increasingly costly attempts to produce tiny gains in forecasting to protecting our environment from the man-made threats which may bring about drastic climate changes.

WHAT I DO: BEHIND-THE-SCENES WEATHER FORECASTING

16

Although I realize the economic value of totally accurate forecasts, I personally enjoy the challenge offered by the unpredictability of weather. My job would turn into dull routine if all I had to do was read a computer printout describing what the weather was guaranteed to be. Instead, I look forward to reporting to work each morning and using my experience and knowledge to provide useful forecasts for my viewers.

Wherever I go (and I go a lot of places—I've visited 46 states and a dozen foreign countries), I get many questions about what my job entails and how I got to be a part of the "Good Morning America" team. So I thought I'd take a little time now to tell you a bit about my career and my daily schedule at ABC.

HOW I GOT HERE

Unlike many of my colleagues in weather reporting, I was not a weather freak as a kid. My interest, like most other people's, was in how the weather affected my daily plans. My obsession was current events, especially the social issues that dominated the 1960s. I was an English major and journalism minor in college, and I saw my first job as a TV reporter in Richmond, Virginia, as the first step toward becoming a network correspondent.

Instead, as I described in the introduction to this book, I was seduced into becoming a weatherman by my general manager, who offered to make me a rich man in Richmond (isn't capitalism grand?). However, once I took the job, I became identified as a personality, and I gained a great deal more attention and exposure than I had in the more limited air time afforded a news reporter. Because winning the ratings war is all-important in television news, I realized that the personality role was my ticket to the big time.

During my three and a half years in Richmond, our local news was number one in the ratings, and I began to get quite a few offers from larger markets. I decided to be patient before I left my secure perch. I turned down, among others, offers from Baltimore

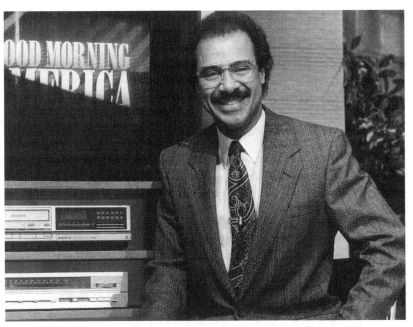

So you think it's easy to smile like this for promotional pictures at 5:00 A.M.?

and New Haven, CT. Then, in early 1975, my Richmond station hired a news director with whom I was less than compatible, so I decided it was time to move on. In a strange coincidence, the news director who had offered me the job in New Haven in 1973 and in Baltimore in 1974 was still looking for a weatherperson in 1975. I called him and said I was ready to move, and he said the job was mine. In July, 1975, with my wife and infant son, I left Richmond for Baltimore.

I felt at home almost immediately, and the audience received me as warmly as if I'd been a native son. Within one year, our ratings had soared to number one. Then, the other stations in town resorted to a time-honored television tactic—they began sending tapes of me and our other personalities to larger markets to get us off the air in Baltimore. I received offers from KNBC in Los Angeles and WABC in New York. Because my wife is a native New Yorker and because I relished the idea of working in the country's largest market, I joined the WABC Eyewitness News team in May 1977. For three years, I did the weather on the 11 P.M. news as well as many feature reports.

By 1980, I was beginning to feel stagnant and intellectually unchallenged because I was limited to doing primarily weather-related stories. So I started bugging the station management to let me do a talk show. Shortly afterward, I was named the host of "Good Morning New York," a one-hour local program that followed

"Good Morning America." Unfortunately, for the first time in my career, my timing stunk. For one thing, I was on directly opposite Phil Donahue, whose ratings were at their peak. For another, the station basically treated the show as a write-off, an opportunity to fill time inexpensively. The show wasn't given the staff or budget to do the kind of program I would have liked to do. And, in all honesty, I must say that I was not mature enough—or assertive enough—to establish myself as a compelling force in the viewers' minds.

Fortunately, after a year, I was rescued. The station's local news ratings had begun to suffer, so I was asked to rejoin the team—this time as a sportscaster. I had been a lifelong sports fan, and over the next five years, I had many dream assignments, including the 1984 Summer Olympics. I had a chance to become friendly with major sports personalities, from Muhammad Ali to Reggie Jackson to George Steinbrenner. Time passed quickly, and I was seldom bored.

My ultimate opportunity resulted from some long-time moonlighting. When I had been a weatherman at WABC, I had often filled in as the weatherman on "Good Morning America" for John Coleman ("GMA" 's original weatherman). I continued to be a regular fill-in throughout my tenure as a talk show host and sportscaster. Then, in 1986, Capital Cities purchased ABC, and the new bosses began a restructuring of "Good Morning America." As part of that restructuring, they asked me to go on "GMA" full-time. My

No, Joan and Charlie didn't buy this cake for the 15th anniversary of my last perfect forecast. Actually, the cake is for the 15th anniversary of "Good Morning America," and one of the few things I don't kid about is my admiration for my two talented colleagues.

job would entail being the regular weatherman, but also filling in as host, doing all kinds of interviews and features, and serving as the traveling good will ambassador for the program.

I couldn't pass up the job, and I've never regretted my decision. Although "GMA" is very demanding on my time and my physical energy, I have the opportunity to communicate, to touch people, in a fashion that is informative and entertaining. In fact, I just might have the best job in television.

MY DAILY SCHEDULE

I couldn't do what I do without a terrific support team, especially my staff meteorologist, Jerry McNiff. The forecasts begin when Jerry arrives at work at 12:30 A.M. and begins plowing through the huge stack of general and local forecasts and maps we receive from the National Weather Service and several private weather forecasting services. From this information, as well as satellite pictures and radar reports, Jerry begins to put together a picture of what the weather is going to be like across the country.

Around 4:00 A.M., about the time I'm stepping out of the shower (I get up at 3:40 A.M.), Jerry places an order with the ABC graphics department for maps and charts. This order normally includes 10 to 14 graphic illustrations, from general-outlook maps to projections of high temperatures across the country to special maps for storms or other severe weather.

These graphics, along with a large stack of weather reports and summaries, are waiting for me when I arrive at 4:50 A.M. As I pore over them, Jerry briefs me on how fast systems are moving, how intense storms are, what paths those storms are likely to take, etc. I like to focus on what is unusual or of special significance in that day's weather. I'll often order more maps or changes in existing maps.

Occasionally, we receive conflicting forecasts for the movement of major storm systems. I'll go over these with Jerry, then I'll apply my two decades of experience and intuition to determine which forecast I'll go with on the air.

I have to be ready by 5:30 A.M., when "ABC's World News This Morning" begins. I do two weather segments in each half hour of this 90-minute program. At 6:42 P.M., after my last segment, I leave the news studio and take the long hike over to the "Good Morning America" studio. On most days, I'm seated with Charlie Gibson and Joan Lunden at 7:00 A.M. when the show begins.

I do one full weather report in each half hour, a weather headline at the top of each hour, and a weather recap at 8:57.

For each report, I stand in front of a "chroma key" panel, a large board painted with a special shade of blue or green. A computerized instrument in the control room automatically superimposes a

For each report, I stand in front of a "chroma key" panel, a large board painted with a special shade of blue or green.

weather map or other graphic when it senses that color. (I have to be careful not to wear clothing that's the same color as the chroma key—if I do, you'll see a thunderstorm on my kneecap and a low pressure system on my shoulder.) To see what you see, I have to glance at a TV monitor off to my side or a monitor mounted on the camera in front of me. I take pride in "working the chroma key" in a way that creates the illusion that I'm touching real maps that are actually behind me.

If you're a regular viewer of "GMA," you know that I'm often sent out to do what we call weather remotes, reports from all over the country. These remotes are often done in conjunction with local events that range from a county fair to Mardi Gras, and they are among favorite aspects of the job. I get to meet a wide variety of interesting people, sample local color and cuisine, and meet the local weatherpeople at our affiliate stations. These local weatherpeople usually join me in a "weather duet," sharing the forecasting job during one of my "GMA" segments. In addition to making friends, I usually pick up a few tips about local weather patterns that may later contribute to the accuracy of my national forecasts.

I also have the opportunity to travel with and without the rest of the GMA team to report on a wide variety of other subjects. Are you beginning to see why I think I have the best job in television?

UNDERSTANDING WEATHER FORECASTS AND MAPS

I've discussed at length how forecasts are prepared and delivered to you. Although the basic elements of the weather in these forecasts have been explained, it's worthwhile to explain and interpret the information you'll find in television, radio, and newspaper weather forecasts. We'll also take a brief look at weather maps.

TEMPERATURE

Most forecasts will give three sets of temperatures:

• The forecast high temperature and low temperature. Unless a front is moving through, the high temperature will be recorded in mid-afternoon, and the low temperature shortly before dawn—a good thing to keep in mind when you're dressing yourself or the kids in the morning.

• The normal high and low temperatures for that date.

• The record high and low temperatures for that date.

In the winter, you will also be given another infamous statistic—the windchill temperature. To understand windchill, remember how our bodies get rid of excess heat—we perspire, and the evaporation of that perspiration cools our skin. Wind increases the rate of evaporation, which is why we hold our hands under blowers in public rest rooms to dry them. In the winter, wind accelerates the loss of heat from our exposed skin, heat we can ill afford to lose. Being outside when the temperature is 10 degrees Fahrenheit is tolerable if there is no wind; but a 20-mile-per-hour wind produces a windchill factor of -25, which brings the danger of frostbite. You should remember that windchill affects only people, pets and other living things, not your automobile or other inanimate objects. (It may take a "pound of flesh" to pay for a car, but the car doesn't have a circulatory system.)

Following is a table that allows you to calculate the windchill factor. The most dangerous conditions occur when the windchill reaches -25 or below.

Wind Speed (mph)	Windchill Temperature						
Calm	40	30	20	10	0	-10	-20
5	37	27	16	6	-5	-15	-26
10	28	16	4	-9	-21	-33	-46
15	22	9	-5	-18	-36	-45	-58
20	18	4	-10	-25	-39	-53	-67
25	16	0	-15	-29	-44	-59	-74
30	13	-2	-18	-33	-48	-63	-79
	40	30	20	10	0	-10	-20

Actual Air Temperature (degrees Fahrenheit)

Wind speeds of more than 30 miles per hour cause very little additional chilling (can you tell the difference between -79 and -81?).

Because meteorologists are such fun-loving and fair people, they wouldn't rest until they had developed another statistic that would tell us how uncomfortable we're going to be in summer, too. This statistic is called the temperature-humidity index, or "humature" (isn't that where you store a cigar?). Anyway, this charming figure is based on the fact that perspiration evaporates much more slowly as the relative humidity rises. You don't need a chart to figure out this statistic—if the temperature-humidity index is over 75, you'll become increasingly uncomfortable.

Some forecasts also provide the mean, or average temperature, which is arrived at by adding the high and low temperatures and dividing by two. In the parts of the United States that have winter weather, the mean temperature is used to compute a statistic called "heating-degree-days."

Here's how it works. You take the mean temperature of the day (let's say 52 degrees) and subtract that from 65 degrees (an arbitrary temperature picked as the point at which a thermostat turns on the furnace in the average home). The result is 13 degree-days. Fuel oil and gas companies use this statistic to calculate, with a high degree of accuracy, how much fuel their customer's furnaces are burning. Most newspapers keep a running total of degree-days in each heating season, comparing it to the normal total and the total for the preceding year. The lower the total degree-days, the warmer the winter, and vice versa.

Honolulu, Hawaii, has never had a heating-degree-day. On the other extreme, states like North Dakota can record more than 12,000 heating-degree-days in a single winter.

HUMIDITY

The "humidity" given in forecasts is really the relative humidity, or the percentage derived from comparing the amount of water vapor the air does contain at a certain temperature with the amount it could hold at the same temperature. If the relative humidity is 66 percent, that means the air holds two-thirds of the water vapor it can hold at that temperature.

Relative humidity does not always reflect how "muggy" or "sticky" the air feels. A relative humidity of 80 percent will be very comfortable when the air temperature is 40 degrees, but will be oppressive when the temperature is 80 degrees.

A better way to estimate comfort is to look at the dew point, or the temperature at which the air could no longer hold the moisture it presently contains. Spencer's Simple Comfort Index says dew points:

Under 40 degrees:	Feel dry to very dry
40–59 degrees:	Feel comfortable
60 degrees or more:	Feel sticky to unbearable.

AIR PRESSURE

Air pressure, or barometric pressure, is usually given in inches of mercury. The average air pressure at sea level is 29.92 inches. Air pressures of 30 inches or more indicate a high-pressure system, while readings below 29.9 indicate a low-pressure system.

The forecast almost always indicates whether the air pressure is rising or falling. Rising pressure generally means increasingly clear weather, while falling pressure means increasing clouds and the possibility of precipitation.

WINDS

Forecasts will include projected wind speed and direction. Although normal winds vary from region to region, a useful rule of thumb is that an "average" wind is ten miles per hour. Speeds above that figure would qualify the day as "windy." A little more detailed guide to wind speeds is:

0–10 miles per hour:	Light or gentle
10–19 miles per hour:	Breezy
20–30 miles per hour:	Strong
30+ miles per hour:	Gale force

Wind direction is often a strong indicator of weather to come.

States like North Dakota can record more than 12,000 heating degree days in a single winter.

For example, in the northeastern United States, west or southwest winds generally bring dry air, south winds bring warm, humid air, and southeast and northeast winds mean stormy weather. After a little observation, you will get to know what kind of weather various winds bring to your area.

SKY CONDITIONS

I explain the terms commonly used to describe sky conditions (partly sunny, overcast, etc.) below. Weather forecasters will often include descriptions of important changes in sky conditions over the forecast periods, such as "increasing cloudiness" or "clearing."

You can get a rough idea of what is going to happen by looking at changes in the sky. The chances for precipitation increase when:

- Isolated clouds thicken, fuse, and lower
- Clouds move from different directions at different times
- A line of middle clouds darkens the horizon
- Heavy, piled-up clouds build to great heights before mid-afternoon
- Clouds develop dark bases

On the other hand, the chances for better weather increase when:

- Fog burns off before noon
- Clouds decrease in number
- Cloud bases become higher
- A sheet of clouds wrinkles up and shows breaks of sunshine

PRECIPITATION

The first precipitation information you'll be given is the total for the last 24 hours, measured in inches. Anything over one-half inch is a lot of rain. The forecast probably won't convert inches of snow to inches of water, but a good rule of thumb is that five or six inches of snow equal one-half inch of rain (remember, cold air holds a lot less water vapor than warm air).

The most confusing of all forecasting terms are those used to describe the likelihood and amounts of rain and snow. Every forecaster has his or her favorite terms, but I'll try to clear up some confusion by defining the ones you'll hear or read most often.

RAIN

The National Weather Service and the Weather Channel commonly use probabilities of rain in their forecasts—for example, a

30-percent chance of rain. This doesn't mean that it will rain 30 percent of the day or that rain will fall on 30 percent of your area. What it means is that the computers have calculated that when conditions have been the same as they are today, at least .01 inch of rain has fallen in the forecast area three out of 10 days.

Because these probabilities are confusing, I prefer the following terminology:

- "Slight chance of precipitation" means there is a 10-percent to 20-percent chance of rain falling.

- "Chance of precipitation" means a 30-percent to 50-percent probability.

- "Occasional precipitation" means that there is a greater-than-50-percent probability that rain will fall, but for less than half of the forecast period.

Forecasts also talk about the duration and geographic distribution of the precipitation. As I said previously, "showers" means brief, localized rainfall, while "rain" means widespread, steadier precipitation. You will hear showers described as:

- "Isolated," which means that less than 10 percent of your area will see any rain.

- "Scattered," which means that 10 percent to 50 percent of the area will get damp.

- "Numerous," which means that most of the area will receive some rain.

"Periods of rain" means that precipitation is likely to fall over the entire area off and on throughout the forecast period.

SNOW

The probabilities of snow are the same as the probabilities of rain; that is, a 30-percent chance of snow means that under similar conditions, snow has fallen on three of 10 days. The terms "slight chance," "chance," and "occasional" mean the same for snow as for rain.

Forecasters also use the following terms:

- "Snow showers" are brief, localized snowfalls. They can be "isolated," "scattered," or "numerous."

- "Snow squalls" are brief but very intense snowfalls in which visibility can be extremely limited.

- "Snow flurries" are very light snowfalls that produce little or no significant precipitation.

"Periods of snow" means widespread precipitation over the forecast region. The intensity of the snow, like the density of fog, is determined by the visibility. If visibility is about a mile, snow is falling at the rate of an inch every two or three hours. If the visibility falls below 5/16ths of a mile, the snow is considered "heavy," with accumulations of an inch per hour or more.

Because snow can produce dangerous travel conditions, the National Weather Service issues a series of alerts:

- "Winter weather advisory" is issued whenever there is the likelihood that snow, sleet, freezing rain, or high winds could make travel difficult. You should continue to monitor weather forecasts if you plan to travel.

- "Winter storm watch" is issued when conditions occur that could lead to a dangerous ice storm or at least six inches of snow. You should eliminate unnecessary travel and prepare for bad weather.

- "Winter storm warning" means that heavy snow or an ice storm is about to begin or has already begun. You should not travel unless absolutely necessary.

Predicting snowfall amounts is one of the most difficult of forecasting tasks because it often comes down to guesswork. Most forecasters prefer to use a figure on the high side so that people aren't caught unprepared. Despite that precaution, every single forecaster (including me!) has seen a forecast for "flurries" turn into a 10-inch snowfall. So you should listen to the radio or television whenever you have winter travel plans.

OTHER INFORMATION

Your local weathercast and the weather page of your local newspaper are also likely to include other interesting or useful information about your area. This information can include:

- Air quality. Our atmosphere can carry bad stuff (pollutants and pollen) along with the good stuff (water vapor, oxygen). In areas where pollution can be a problem (most cities), the weather forecast often includes a rating of air quality (from good to

Winter storm watch is issued when conditions occur that could lead to a dangerous ice storm or at least six inches of snow.

unhealthy), along with information about what pollutants are causing the problem (ozone, carbon monoxide, sulfur dioxide, etc.). Allergy sufferers (who "nose" how many there are?) often find out if there are pollens, mold spores, or anything else to sneeze at in the air.

• Marine forecasts and information. Because almost two-thirds of all Americans live within 50 miles of our nation's coast, most of you receive forecasts that include times of high and low tides, projected wind speeds and direction, projected wave heights, and range of visibility. Every National Weather Service office near the coast has staff that constantly monitor marine weather conditions so that small craft advisories and other warnings can be issued. The U.S. Coast Guard provides special telephone weather information for boaters.

• Aviation forecasts and information. Your general weather forecasts provide information on the height of the clouds (ceiling) and visibility. The U.S. Weather Service also monitors aviation weather and maintains a local or toll-free telephone service that provides detailed weather information for pilots.

• Traveler's forecasts. The best way to find out what the weather's going to be like at your destination is to watch me on "World News This Morning" or "Good Morning America." If it's the weekend, your local paper probably lists the forecast high and low temperatures and weather conditions for major United States and foreign cities.

• Sun, moon, stars and planets. Your forecasts usually include the times of sunrise and sunset, the phase of the moon (useful to lovers and werewolves), and, occasionally, information about stars, planets and other interesting sights in the skies.

WEATHER MAPS

One of the most difficult tasks I faced when I became a weatherman was learning to identify each U.S. state from its outline on the national weather map immediately, at first glance. So I'd stand there talking about a tornado sweeping through Nebraska while I was pointing at South Dakota or Kansas. (I think all geography buffs are sprinters—you wouldn't believe how quickly people who noticed my gaffes got to the phone!)

After 20 years, I'm a whiz at U.S. states and cities (no one can say I'm not a fast learner). And that's important, because weather maps are as important to weatherpeople as videotape replays are to sportscasters. Interesting, well-designed weather maps provide pictures of national and local weather conditions that are worth far more than a thousand words (and that's important, because I barely have time for a couple hundred words on each of my "GMA" forecasts).

Producing well-designed and informative maps is a big job, because the maps we receive from the National Weather Service are about as easy to decipher as the schematic drawing of the circuit boards of your television set. My job is to strip out all the chicken scratching (even though meteorologists may cry "foul") and produce simple maps that provide, at a glance, a snapshot of what the weather will be like in your area and in other parts of the country.

On my reports, and on your local weathercasts, you're likely to see the following types of information presented on U.S. maps:

• Location of the jet stream(s). Jet steams serve as the highways of world weather. A map showing the jet stream provides a good picture of the paths major weather systems are likely to take.

• Location of fronts and highs and lows. The symbols for fronts used on almost all weather maps are:

Cold front ▼▼▼▼

Warm front ●●●●

Stationary front ▼▲▼▲

Highs are indicated by a H and lows by L

• *Precipitation.* On television, we normally use color to indicate areas of precipitation—for example, shades of green to indicate rain and shades of red to indicate snow. In newspapers, various symbols are used, such as diagonal lines for rain.

• *Temperature.* We use bands of color to indicate the projected high temperatures of the day, with each band representing a range of ten degrees (for example, 50s, 60s, 70s, etc.) Newspapers use lines to separate the bands.

• *Barometric pressure.* Meteorologists draw lines surrounding areas of equal air pressure. These lines are called "isobars." Isobars are shown on some newspaper weather maps; if you'd like to impress a friend with your weather knowledge, point out that the closer together the isobars, the stronger the winds. (Remember, air flows from high pressure to low pressure—the big-

ger the difference, the faster the winds.) By the way, there is no
truth to the rumor that Eskimos hang out at isobars!

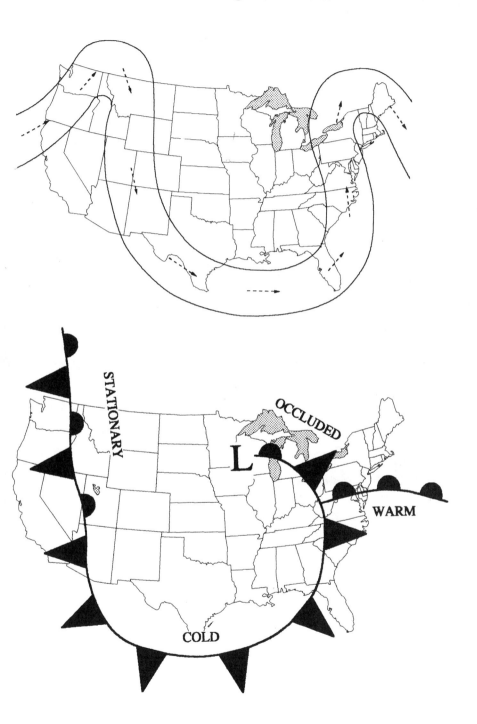

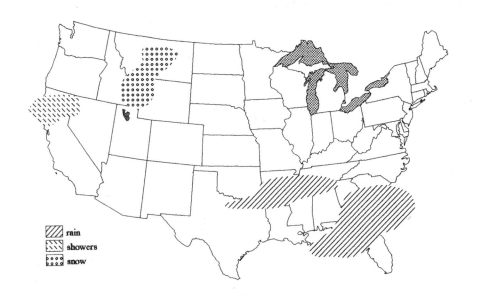

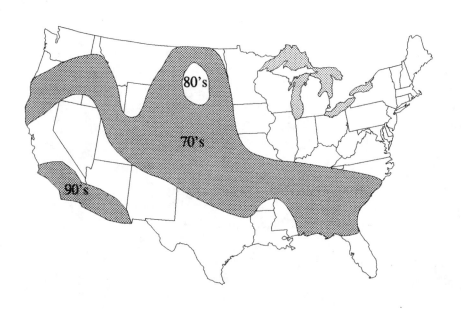

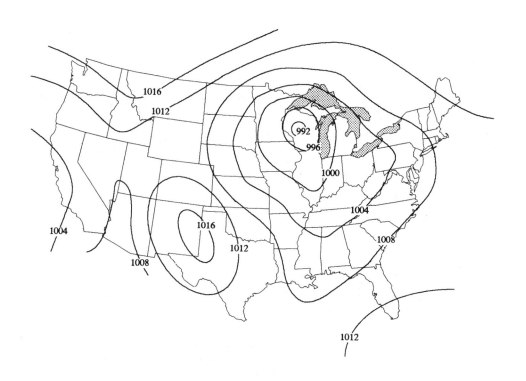

FROM TUNDRA TO TROPICS: A GUIDE TO THE CLIMATES OF THE WORLD

18

We human beings are very adaptable creatures, and we can find ways to survive almost anywhere on our planet, from the frozen tundra of the far north to the blazing, arid deserts of the Middle East. But there's a much more limited selection of areas in which large numbers of us can live in relative comfort and in which we can support ourselves. If we could somehow transport Chicago to the location of Nome, Alaska, that city would soon wither down to a few thousand people. Perhaps the most important factor in where large numbers of us have settled and continued to live is not weather, but climate.

The difference between weather and climate is time: Weather is what happens today or this week; climate is our environment over years, decades, or more. Weather is full of bizarre and extreme events—80-degree-days in Minneapolis in January, snow in New York in July. Even years can be abnormal: Some northern cities have recorded 10 times more snowfall one year than the preceding year. But when weather events are averaged over the course of many years, a more accurate picture of the level of rainfall, precipitation, percentage of sunshine, and other events in that area emerges. It's useful to think about weather and climate as the difference between a baseball player's performance over a few games and his performance over his entire career. A player can go 0 for 25 in a week or hit .500; he can even put together a fantastic or an utterly miserable season. But his statistics over his career are what will classify him as a Hall of Famer or a utility player.

I'm on the air every weekday morning talking about the weather, a subject that is the immediate concern of my audience. But as a veteran journalist, I am acutely aware that our world is increasingly becoming one global village. In this global village, climate has an impact on the political, economic, and social trends and events that affect us in the United States. Climate is also a barometer of the health of our vital but fragile worldwide environment. That's why all of us should have a basic understanding of climates around the world.

WHAT ELEMENTS MAKE UP CLIMATE?

The word *climate* comes from the Greek word *klima*, meaning "region" or "zone." When our old friend Aristotle put his great mind to classifying the long-term weather in different parts of his world, he concentrated only on one element: Temperature. The famous Greek philosopher decided that the world was divided into three climate zones based on temperature: torrid, temperate, and frigid.

Aristotle's theory was accepted until the last three centuries, when men of scientific bent discovered the composition of air, measured air pressure, explored the nature and importance of cloud formation, and measured and analyzed wind patterns. By the 19th century, scientists realized that climate was determined not only by temperature, but by precipitation, humidity, wind patterns, air pressure, and degree of cloudiness. Of these factors, temperature and precipitation are the most important.

HOW DO WE TALK ABOUT TEMPERATURE?

Two temperature statistics are important in determining climate: annual mean temperature and annual temperature range. To compute the annual mean temperature, we first have to compute the mean, or average daily temperature. This is simply the average of the high temperature and the low temperature recorded over a 24-hour period. For example, if the high were 70 degrees and the low were 50 degrees, we would compute the average by adding the two together (120) and dividing by two to arrive at a daily mean temperature of 60 degrees. The annual mean temperature is the average of all 365 daily temperatures. The average annual mean temperature over the entire globe is 59 degrees Fahrenheit.

The annual temperature range is the difference between the lowest monthly mean temperature and the highest monthly mean temperature. In the United States, the temperature range over the year can be under 10 degrees (in places like San Francisco) to more than 40 degrees (in Chicago or Minneapolis). Temperature range has as much effect on an area's plant and animal life and suitability for agriculture as does the average annual mean temperature.

HOW DO WE TALK ABOUT PRECIPITATION?

Two precipitation statistics are also important: Total annual precipitation and the distribution of precipitation during the year.

The word climate comes from the Greek word klima, meaning "region" or "zone."

Total precipitation figures range from 80 inches or more in tropical rain forests to less than 10 inches in deserts and the polar regions.

How much rain falls at one time and when during the year it falls can be just as crucial to plant life and agriculture as total rainfall. For example, parts of the United States Plains have a relatively low annual precipitation, but much of it falls in late May, June, and July—the vital period for crop growth. Certain desert areas, such as parts of Arizona, occasionally experience torrential rainfalls, but much of it runs off or evaporates, making it useless for agriculture.

HOW DO TEMPERATURE AND PRECIPITATION COMBINE TO FORM CLIMATES?

In the 19th century, several systems of climate classifications were developed, including some that divided our planet into as many as 35 different zones. Then, in 1900, Wladimir Koppen, a German meteorologist, made the observation that the vegetation that grew in specific areas was directly related to the variations of temperature and precipitation in those areas. Over a career that spanned 50 years, he refined a system that divided the land areas of the world into climate regions based on the relationship between temperature, precipitation, and plant life. This system featured five major climate types, which Koppen labeled "A" through "E":

A. Tropical (hot) rainy climates
B. Dry climates
C. Humid moderate temperature climates
D. Humid cold climates
E. Polar climates

WHAT DETERMINES THE DISTRIBUTION OF THESE CLIMATES?

Aristotle believed that latitude, or the distance from the equator, was the only factor that determined annual temperature. But since we've read the first section of this book, we know better. Although latitude does obviously play a part in climate (the equator gets a lot more solar energy than the north pole), the annual temperatures and precipitation in an area also depend greatly on:

• Geography—the location of landmasses, oceans, lakes, rivers, and mountains.

• Global wind patterns and ocean currents.

• The location of semi-permanent air masses, highs, and lows.

Keep these factors in mind while we talk about Koppen's climate areas.

TROPICAL RAINY CLIMATES

In these areas of the world, the mean temperature for any month never falls below 64 degrees Fahrenheit, so there is no winter. Tropical rainy climates can be divided into:

- *Rain Forest:* These hot, rainy, oppressively humid areas have no dry season—precipitation in every month is greater than 2.4 inches. Rain forests feature giant trees with heavy undergrowth. This climate predominates in lands closest to the equator, such the Amazon and Congo river basins.

- *Monsoon:* Monsoon comes from an Arabic word meaning "season," but it's now used by meteorologists to describe a wind pattern that reverses with the seasons. For example, in winter, northeasterly winds bring warm, dry air to much of the Indian subcontinent. But in the spring, as the northern hemisphere tilts toward the sun, the winds reverse, bringing great amounts of moisture from the Indian Ocean which fall as heavy rains for at least six months. Much of Southeast Asia also has a monsoon climate.

- *Savannah:* This word refers to treeless plains or relatively flat grasslands that serve as the transitional areas between equatorial rain forests and deserts. Savannahs receive heavy rains during part of the year, but they also have a well-defined dry season. They feature very tall (as high as 10-inch) grasses, but few tall trees. Savannah areas include the veldts of Africa, the plains of central and eastern India, the *campos* of Brazil, and southern Florida.

Monsoon comes from an Arabic word meaning "season," but it's now used by meteorologists to describe a wind pattern that reverses with the seasons.

DRY CLIMATES

Dry climates are those in which the annual rainfall is less than the annual loss of water through evaporation. There are two basic types of dry climates:

- *Steppes* are semi-arid areas that occur in tropical, subtropical, and mid-latitude areas. These areas have less than 20 inches of annual rainfall, almost all of which falls during a short wet season. Grass grows quickly when it rains, but it becomes dry and wiry the rest of the time. Bushes exist, but few trees. Large steppe areas include central Mexico, west central Asia, northwest Africa, and a narrow band of U.S. land east of the Rocky Mountains.

• Deserts feature very little annual rainfall and sparse vegetation. Most of the world's great deserts, including Africa's Sahara Desert, Asia's Gobi Desert, and the deserts of the American Southwest are in the horse latitudes, where currents warm the air and dissipate clouds as they descend from the upper atmosphere. Other desert areas are created in the shadow of tall mountain ranges that block moisture-laden winds. One such desert at the base of the Andes Mountains in Chile includes areas that have recorded no rainfall over the last half century.

HUMID MODERATE CLIMATES

These mid-latitude areas feature adequate annual rainfall and mild winters, with the mean temperature for the coldest month falling between 27 degrees Fahrenheit and 64 degrees Fahrenheit. These climates fall into four major categories:

• *Mediterranean:* These areas have warm, dry summers, with at least three times as much rainfall in the wettest winter month as in the driest summer month. Mediterranean climates obviously include the countries bordering on that sea, along with southern California, Cape Province of South Africa, and much of southern Australia.

• *Cool, dry summers:* The average temperature never exceeds 72 degrees in any month, but for at least four months the average temperature is at least 50 degrees. Again, rainfall in winter averages three times the summer precipitation. Among the areas with this climate are Portugal and the northern California coast.

• *Humid, warm summers:* The average temperature for the warmest months is more than 72 degrees, and rainfall is plentiful year-round. The favorable temperatures and copious rainfall provide perfect conditions for agriculture. These areas include much of Uruguay, Paraguay, southern Brazil and the southeastern United States.

• *Marine West Coast:* The significant feature of this climate is year-round temperatures that vary less from month to month than the other three climate areas in this classification. Precipitation is also plentiful during the cool summers and mild winters. These areas include the British Isles, the west coast of France, the southeast coast of South Africa, and New Zealand.

HUMID COLDER CLIMATES

The difference between these climates and the Humid Moderate Climates is that the mean temperature falls below 27 degrees at least one month of the year. As a result, the winters can be classified as severe rather than mild.

• *Humid, warm summers:* These areas, which have at least one month with average temperatures above 72 degrees, feature precipitation spread out all through the year, with no real dry season. This climate includes vast areas of fertile agricultural lands in the northern United States, southern Canada, Europe, and Asia.

• *Cool, dry winters:* Summers in these zones are cooler, with an average temperature less than 72 degrees in the warmest month. Because these areas are swept by polar air masses during the winter, the weather is very dry and severely cold. This climate includes north central Canada and vast expanses of northeastern Asia.

POLAR CLIMATES

In these arctic and near arctic areas, no month has an average temperature of more than 50 degrees. As a result, there is no summer and no trees grow. The two types of polar climates are:

• *Tundra:* These areas represent the world's youngest climate, because the ice sheets from the last ice age retreated from them as recently as 7,000 years ago. As a result, the Earth is covered with very little soil and few species have had time to adapt. The average temperature does struggle above 32 degrees in summer, so some mosses, lichens, and berry-bearing bushes manage to grow. Tundra borders the polar ice cap throughout the northern hemisphere.

• *Ice Cap:* The average temperature never rises above 32 degrees, so these areas have permanent snow and ice.

HOW PERMANENT ARE THESE CLIMATES?

Although the climate where we live seems little changed in our lifetimes, the global climate is changing all the time. While we tend to think of the Earth today as a benevolent, mild place, our climate is in fact marked by much greater extremes of heat and cold than have been typical over the last 500 million years. For example, polar ice caps have existed for less than 10 percent of that vast stretch of time. Global warming is nothing new in the history of the Earth.

However, warming and other climate changes that take place over very short periods of time are matters of great concern.

Our climate is in fact marked by much greater extremes of heat and cold than have been typical over the last 500 million years.

A CORNUCOPIA OF CLIMATES: THE RICH DIVERSITY OF U.S. WEATHER

19

Of all the climates in the world, the one we're all most concerned about is the climate where we live. If you look at weather as a series of theatrical events, the United States is the world's "Broadway," a stage for the world's most interesting weather. Mark Twain once described New England as a place with 134 different kinds of weather—all of which took place on the same day. Although the great humorist was exaggerating a bit (as we humorists tend to do), his comment does emphasize that our country is a jigsaw of climate types that display the richest possible diversity of weather events.

As I said before, the key elements of climate are temperature and precipitation. And the patterns in which these elements occur depend in turn on three basic factors:

• The prevailing winds and ocean currents

• The location of semi-permanent air masses and high-and-low-pressure systems.

• Geography: the location of our continent, mountain ranges, oceans, lakes, and plains.

Previously, I've explained the prevailing winds, ocean currents, and the meanderings of the jet stream. I've also described the semi-permanent air masses and highs and lows that generate our weather. But before we talk about climate, I have to spend a little time talking about the geography of our continent.

GEOGRAPHY: MEET NORTH AMERICA

Any of you who have endured windchills of 40 degrees below zero when an Arctic high dips into the United States, or have experienced the terror of hurricanes storming in from the Caribbean have no doubt uttered a profound wish that weather would stop at the U.S. borders. But weather doesn't pay the slightest bit of attention to lines drawn on a map. To understand the geography of our weather, we have to take a look at North America and its surroundings.

The North American continent today is entirely in the northern hemisphere, stretching from just north of the equator at the tip of Central America to the Arctic Ocean in the far north. Because it stretches almost the entire distance from the equator to the North Pole, you might say that nature gave North America a lot of latitude (no dobut a lot more than you're likely to give me). You'll realize how far south our continent stretches when you consider that a line parallel to the equator running through the southernmost point of North America, which would also run through Nigeria, pass south of the entire Arabian peninsula, touch the southern tip of India, and run right through Ho Chi Minh City (the former Saigon), Viet Nam.

North America, at 9,406,000 square miles, is the third-largest continent. It's a little more than half the size of Asia, about 20 percent smaller than Africa and 25 percent larger than South America. The northern border of North America stretches 4,100 miles, but the southern border is barely 30 miles wide.

To us humans, nothing seems more fixed and permanent than the massive continents. But as I mentioned earlier in this book, continents are really blocks of lighter rocks such as granite that float like boats in a bathtub on the plastic-like mantle below. In the last 4 billion years, the block that we call North America has wandered all over the globe, floating as far north as the North Pole and reaching south below the equator.

North America began as a series of massive volcanoes spewing forth thick sheets of lava that formed a Y-shaped landmass that extended from about the present Great Lakes region northward, splitting into a Y around the present Hudson Bay. Over the course of 1.5 billion years, the volcanoes eroded to a virtually flat plain, and the sediment from that erosion built up land upon its flanks.

While this erosion was taking place, baby North America was picking up pieces of land as it drifted around the globe. About 1.9 billion years ago, the continents slammed together into one large continent, and the collision produced a huge mountain chain in northern Canada that has also since eroded. At one point about this time, North America straddled the North Pole.

The continent broke free, only to come together again about 600 million years ago with what is now Europe, Greenland, and parts of Asia. In the process it collided with a smaller landmass about 570 million years ago to raise the mountains of New England; 120 million years later, another collision produced the rest of the

The northern border of North America stretches 4,100 miles, but the southern border is barely 30 miles wide.

Appalachian Mountain chain. While this was going on, North America was straddling the equator, which is why remnants of ancient coral reefs are found today in the central United States.

While North America was basking in the tropical sun, what are now South America and Africa were covered in thick ice sheets at the South Pole. When the continents moved northward, the ice sheets melted, raising sea levels to the point where much of North America was either totally submerged or covered with marshes and swamps. The inland seas left seashells in Montana; the decaying vegetation from swamps and marshes became America's vast coal and oil deposits.

Finally, about 200 million years ago, North America pulled apart from Europe to begin the formation of the Atlantic Ocean. It drifted north and west until about 70 million years ago, when it collided with the Pacific plate. This collision raised the Rocky Mountains and added land that became California and the other western states. At about the same time, in other parts of the world, similar collisions were raising the Himalayas, the Alps, the Andes, and the Atlas mountains.

GEOGRAPHY AND OUR WEATHER— A BROAD OVERVIEW

This short travelogue of North America is more than just interesting; the sequence of the wanderings and collisions has a profound affect on our weather. If the collision that formed the mountains across Canada had occurred 70 million years ago rather than 1.9 billion years ago, the tall peaks of this chain would have served as a barrier against the cold Arctic air masses. If the Appalachian Chain had formed more recently, the Northeastern and Mid-Atlantic states might have a Mediterranean climate with palm trees instead of pines.

But, of course, this didn't happen. So we're stuck with this basic configuration: a landmass sandwiched between two oceans with a large body of warm, moist tropical air to the southeast.

Pacific air moving onshore makes much of the West Coast the cloudiest and dampest part of the United States. But all this moisture falls from the clouds when the air slams into the Rocky Mountains. The western half of the interior United States lies in the "rain shadow" of the mountains, making it the driest part of the country.

The vast central plain of North America is a battleground for the year-round clashes of warm, moist air moving northward and cool, dry air moving southward. In the winter, cold air from northern Canada and the Arctic dominates. The north-central part of the United States has very cold and relatively dry winters; the southern states have less-severe winters and more precipitation.

The vast central plain of North America is a battleground for the year-round clashes of warm, moist air moving northward and cool, dry air moving southward.

In the summer, the warm air pushes northward, bringing thunderstorms and other violent weather with it. If the edge of the warm air pushes unusually far northward into Canada, record heat and drought can punish the central United States.

The eastern states, from Florida to New England, have substantial moisture year-round, thanks to storm systems moving northward up the coast from the Gulf of Mexico and the Caribbean and "northeasters" moving southwest from the Icelandic low. The Atlantic Ocean moderates the climate of New England and the Mid-Atlantic states, giving them less-severe winters than the northern plains.

OUR SEASONS

Astronomically, our seasons in the northern hemisphere are defined by the orbit of the Earth around the sun: Winter begins on December 21, when the sun is at its southernmost point; summer on June 21, when the sun reaches its northernmost point; spring and fall begin on the two equinoxes, March 21 and September 21. Meteorologically, though, the seasons are defined by average temperatures. Winter is the coldest season of the year, and by December 21, much of the northern United States is two or three weeks into the season. On the other hand, by the same definition, winter is generally over by March 1, three weeks before astronomical spring.

To understand the climate of the United States, it's useful to take a look at the meteorological seasons across the country.

• *Winter.* Another common definition of the beginning of winter is the date on which the average daily temperature drops below freezing. This can be as early as the first 10 days of November for North Dakota and northwest Minnesota, the last 10 days of November for New England, Upstate New York and the Upper Midwest, and December 15 for the Mid-Atlantic states and much of the Midwest. The average daily temperature never drops below 32 degrees Fahrenheit in much of the South and the Pacific Coast, so those regions don't have winter (by this definition) at all.

A third marker for the coming of winter is the first snowfall. Flakes can be spotted in the Rocky Mountains in late September, late October or early November in the Northern Plains and mountains of New England, and by late November or early December in other areas where the average daily temperature falls below 32 degrees.

• *Spring.* This season marks the end of winter. Average daily temperatures climb above 32 degrees. For most of the country that has winter, this occurs between late February and the second week of March.

Those people with a botanical bent define spring as the time when the average high temperature reaches 50 degrees, the point at which plant life wakes from its winter sleep. By this definition, spring arrives about the first of February in the South and as late as May 1 in the northern United States.

• *Summer*. If you define summer as the hottest season of the year, it begins somewhere between late May and June 15. The peak summer normally begins about a month after the first day of the season.

Summer can also be defined as the season during which average daily temperatures top 68 degrees. This plateau is reached by May 1 in most of the South, by June 1 across the central United States, and by June 15 in the northern United States. However, some parts of the Pacific Coast and some mountainous areas don't have any summer by this definition.

• *Autumn*. If you consider autumn the three months in between the hottest and coldest quarters, then it begins in most of the United States between the last week in August and the first week in September. The exception is much of the California coast, where warm temperatures persist as late as September 30.

If, on the other hand, you consider the start of fall when the average daily temperatures drop below 68 degrees, summer ends in late August in the northern states, in September in the central United States, and well into October in the southern states.

THE WEATHER FROM SEA TO SEA: REGIONAL CLIMATES OF THE CONTINENTAL UNITED STATES

Geography, wind patterns, the location of semi-permanent air masses, highs, and lows, and the movement of the sun all combine to determine the climate where you live. Since most U.S. weather moves from west to east, we'll go in the same direction in explaining a little bit about regional climates.

• *The Pacific Northwest*. Washington, Oregon, the California coast from San Francisco northward, and parts of Idaho share a climate that features the smallest annual range of temperatures in the United States. Because this area is dominated by Pacific Maritime air, it has mild winters and only moderately warm temperatures. A mixture of clouds and fog makes it the least sunny region of the United States. Its climate is very similar to that of Great Britain and northwest Europe.

The Pacific Northwest has precipitation all year, but winter is the wettest season. In the summer, the Pacific High expands, directing major storm systems northward; the U.S. coast is often foggy but seldom rainy. Seattle, Washington, averages just 2.7 inches of precipitation in June, July, and August, less than half the average 5.6 inches that falls in December.

The lack of temperature contrast means that the Pacific Northwest experiences very little violent weather—thunderstorms are infrequent and tornadoes very rare. A combination of prevailing westerly winds and the cool waters of the Pacific prevents tropical depressions from reaching this region.

• *California.* Except for the slice of northern coast, California has a Mediterranean climate featuring very dry summers and wetter winters. In the summer, California bakes as the strong Pacific high keeps clouds away—Los Angeles averages only .3 inch of precipitation from May through September. The cool Pacific current that flows southward keeps summer temperatures moderate along the coast, but the average daily high temperatures soar to 116 degrees inland in Death Valley.

In the winter, when the Pacific High shrinks, low-pressure systems move in from the Pacific Northwest, bringing heavy snowfalls to the mountains and rain to the coast and inland valleys. Winter temperatures remain mild.

California experiences relatively few thunderstorms and very infrequent tornadoes. Tropical cyclones seldom reach California at hurricane strength. However, because the soil of this semi-arid area is so hard-packed, tropical storms and other systems that bring heavy rains can cause extensive flooding and damaging mud slides.

• *The Southwest.* Arizona, Nevada, and New Mexico are part of the great Western Cordillera, the mountain ranges and plateaus that stretch from the Mexican border into Canada. Because these states are dominated by persistent high pressure and because they are in the rain shadow of the California mountains to the west, annual precipitation is very low. The southwestern states are the sunniest region of the country, and the low humidity makes the climate a healthy one for people suffering from respiratory distress.

The yearly temperature range depends on altitude. Summer high temperatures average in the hundreds in Phoenix at an altitude of 1,100 feet, but reach a maximum of 80 degrees at Sante Fe, which has an altitude of 7,000 feet.

Lack of precipitation means little violent weather. The most dangerous weather condition is flooding caused by heavy rainfall from the occasional tropical storm moving northward from Mexico.

• *The northern Rocky Mountains.* The climate of Colorado,

Except for the slice of northern coast, California has a Mediterranean climate featuring very dry summers and wetter winters.

Utah, Montana, Wyoming, and most of Idaho is colder and wetter than that in the mountain states to the south. But because most of the moisture from Pacific air falls on the Cascades, annual precipitation averages less than 20 inches per year over most of the area, and some plateaus are actually deserts or semi-arid.

The region is relatively sunny. Great temperature swings from day to day are relatively common—October temperatures in Cheyenne, Wyoming, range from a record high of 85 degrees to a record low of 5 degrees below zero.

Thunderstorms caused by the lifting of moist air as it hits the mountains are relatively frequent. Tornadoes, on the other hand, are relatively rare.

- *The Great Plains and northern Midwest*. This vast region of the United States (which includes North Dakota, South Dakota, Minnesota, Wisconsin, Michigan, Kansas, Nebraska, Missouri, Illinois, Indiana, Ohio, Iowa, and Kentucky) has a true continental climate, featuring severe winters and warm, humid summers. In the winter, the weather is dominated by bitterly cold, dry air moving southward from northern Canada and the Arctic. These cold fronts, often called "Alberta clippers," drop little precipitation—except when they pick up moisture crossing the Great Lakes and dump it as heavy "lake-effect" snows on the opposite shores. (That's why areas like Buffalo, New York, record such high annual snowfall totals.) The occasional widespread snowstorm generally begins as a strong low-pressure system carried southeastward from the Pacific Northwest by a trough in the jet stream. These storms cross the Rocky Mountains, pick up moisture from the Gulf of Mexico, then are carried back northward by the jet stream.

In the spring and early summer, warm, moist Gulf air moves northward, spawning violent thunderstorms and tornadoes as it clashes with the retreating cold artic air. Most of the precipitation in this region is produced by thunderstorms. The total annual precipitation is 16 to 32 inches per year in the western half (the area farthest from the Gulf and closest to the rain-blocking western mountains) and 32 to 48 inches in the eastern half.

The north-central United States is prone to prolonged periods of drought. The severe summer drought of 1988 resulted when a huge persistent high-pressure system anchored itself over central Canada and the northern United States, steering Pacific storms northward into Canada and preventing moist Gulf air from moving northward.

- *The south-central and Gulf states*. Warm, moist Gulf air dominates this lower half of the central U.S., which includes the states of Oklahoma, Arkansas, Tennessee, Texas, Louisiana, Mississippi, and Alabama. Although Arctic air occasionally forces its way down into the region, winter temperatures in the region rarely average below freezing for any month of the year. Summers are slightly warmer than those in the north central United States, but they last much longer and are sandwiched by much warmer springs and falls.

Precipitation over the area generally averages 40 to 50 inches per year (the exception is western Texas and Oklahoma). Summer is the wettest season, but precipitation falls year around. The regional climate is generally sunny, but the average relative humidity is significantly higher than it is in the southwestern or Rocky Mountain states.

This region is home to more violent weather—thunderstorms, tornadoes and hurricanes—than any other region of the country.

• *The southern Atlantic states.* The climate of this region, which includes Florida, Georgia, South Carolina, North Carolina, Virginia, and West Virginia, features hot, damp summers and mild winters. Arctic air can bring below-freezing temperatures as far south as northern Florida, but such incursions are rarer than they are in the south-central United States.

No part of this region averages less than 32 inches of precipitation per year, with several areas averaging over 60 inches. In the summer, much of the precipitation falls from frequent thunderstorms that form in late afternoon. The southern half of the region averages less than 1 inch of snow per year, while the northern half averages under 10 inches.

The thunderstorms in this area spawn tornadoes, but they tend to be weak. Far more dangerous and destructive are hurricanes, such as Andrew (which devasted South Florida) and Hugo (which slammed into the Charleston, South Carolina area).

• *The Mid-Atlantic and New England states.* The climate in this region, which includes New York, New Jersey, Pennsylvania, Delaware, Maryland, Connecticut, Massachusetts, Rhode Island, Vermont, New Hampshire, and Maine, is wetter and more moderate than that of the north-central United States. The summers are hot but less humid than other regions east of the Rockies—thunderstorms are significantly less frequent than they are in the north-central, south-central, and south Atlantic states. Winters are quite long in the northern half of this region, but the air temperatures and windchill factors seldom plummet to the bitter depths of those reached in the Upper Midwest.

Annual precipitation averages 40 to 60 inches, and is evenly distributed throughout the year. Upstate New York, western Massachusetts, Vermont, New Hampshire, and Maine average more than 60 inches of snow per year—more than any other areas of the country except northern Michigan and the highest elevations of the western mountains. Unpleasant mixes of snow, sleet, freezing rain, and rain often plague the southern half of this region.

Devastating thunderstorms and tornadoes are relatively infrequent in this area, but hurricanes moving up the coast have caused significant destruction.

ALASKA—A CORNUCOPIA OF CLIMATES

Alaska is the largest American state, covering an area more than twice the size of Texas. It stretches east-west across three time zones and north-south across an expanse as long as the distance from El Paso, Texas, to the Canadian border. Much of this state is covered by mountains that include some of the highest peaks in North America. Large glaciers descend from these mountains almost to sea level.

The interior and north coast of Alaska have an arctic or subartic climate. Barrow, on the shores of the Arctic Ocean, is icebound for most of the year. The average daily high in Barrow is below zero four months of the year and is above freezing only four months of the year. Fairbanks, which is representative of inland Alaska, has a long, bitterly cold winter. However, because of the long hours of daylight, the Fairbanks summer is surprisingly warm, with the average high temperature reaching 72 degrees in July. Because the air is too cold to hold significant moisture, northern and interior Alaska receive very little precipitation.

Anchorage, which is located in a sheltered bay on the southern coast, has much warmer winters than inland regions. Average winter temperatures approximate those of Minneapolis. However, ocean waters keep summer temperatures quite cool—the average daily high in July is just 65 degrees. Precipitation in Alaska is frequent but light.

The Aleutian Islands experience a very narrow range of temperatures year around. On an average December day on the island of Atka, the high temperature is 37 and the low is 30; on the average July day, the high is 57 and the low is 46. Rainfall is plentiful year-round.

HAWAII—THE WEATHERMAN'S PARADISE

The best way to sum up the weather forecast for a tropical area is: "The weather tomorrow will be the same as the weather today." The television stations in Hawaii, which has a tropical climate, don't have regular weathermen on their news broadcasts. "Sunny, warm, with a chance of an afternoon shower" will do it for almost every day of the year. Honolulu has never had a heating-degree-

The best way to sum up the weather forecast for a tropical area is: "The weather tomorrow will be the same as the weather today."

day (which means the average temperature for a day has never fallen below 65 degrees) and has never seen a flake of snow.

Precipitation does vary from location to location. Moist air blowing in off the Pacific hits some volcanic mountains, dropping large volumes of precipitation that have reached over 700 inches per year. Other areas, in the rain shadows of these mountains, get as little as 12 to 20 inches per year.

WILD AND WONDERFUL WEATHER: FASCINATING STATISTICS AND TRIVIA

20

When you're really interested in a subject, whether it's baseball, politics, or the weather, you love trivia and statistics. And because sophisticated instruments constantly monitor atmospheric conditions all over the world, weather buffs have a particularly large treasure trove of facts to feast on. For your enjoyment, I've accumulated information on some of the most interesting and bizarre weather ever recorded.

I do have to point out that the operative expression is "ever recorded." Considering that the Earth is 4.5 billion years old, the length of time that we humans have been capable of accurately measuring temperature, precipitation, and other phenomena is incredibly brief. For example, the weather in Antarctica has been consistently monitored only since 1957. That means that more extreme weather than these listed records may well have occurred—and, more importantly, may occur again.

HIGHEST AND LOWEST RECORDED TEMPERATURES

You might think that the world's hottest temperatures would be recorded at the equator, where the sun's rays shine most strongly year around. But equatorial regions of the Earth are covered by rain forests, and the combination of vegetation, precipitation, and cloud cover keep the temperatures from soaring. Instead, the hottest parts of the world are deserts in the temperate zone. The world and U.S. records are:

World record: 136 degrees Fahrenheit, El Azizia, Libya, September 13, 1922

U.S. record :   134 degrees Fahrenheit, Death Valley, California, July 10, 1913

If hanging out by a foundry furnace is your idea of a blast, then plan your next vacation for Death Valley. This 140-mile-long, 6-mile-wide stretch of paradise has the highest summer temperatures in the world—daily highs average 116 in July, and nightime lows are sometimes over 100. However, when the sun heads south in the fall, the temperatures in Death Valley plummet. The highest year-round average temperature in the continental United States is the 78 degrees recorded in Key West, Florida, the southernmost point in the contiguous 48 states. The highest year-round average in the world is 88 degrees, at Lugh, Somalia, in East Africa. And when it comes to heat waves, comfort yourself with the knowledge you weren't living in Marble Bar, Australia, between October 30, 1923 and April 7, 1924, when the thermometer registered 100 degrees or more for 162 consecutive days.

It probably doesn't come as a huge surprise that Antarctica holds the world record for the lowest temperature. In fact, that frigid reading is a whopping 39 degrees lower than the lowest temperature recorded on any other continent (-90 degrees, Siberia, 1933). In another garden spot on the southernmost continent, Plateau Station, the average annual mean temperature is -70 degrees. By comparison, Barrow, Alaska, with an average annual mean temperature of 9 degrees, seems like a tropical paradise. (You bring the suntan oil, I'll bring the volleyball.)

In the lower 48 states, Butte, Montana, may be the coldest city—it averages 223 days per year with below-freezing temperatures. Another Montana city, Havre, may have experienced the nation's longest sustained cold snap when it recorded below-zero temperatures for 400 consecutive hours. The most severe cold wave may have occurred in February 1899, when the Mississippi River froze all the way from its source to its mouth, with 2-inch-thick ice clogging the harbor at New Orleans.

The world and U.S. lowest temperature records are:

World record: -129 degrees, Vostok, Antarctica, July 21, 1983

U.S. record :   -80 degrees, Prospect Creek, Alaska,
                 January 23, 1971

U.S. record :   -70 degrees, Rogers Pass, Montana,
                 (Ex. Alaska)January 20, 1954

If you're looking for a question that is guaranteed to stump any nonmeteorologist (and maybe even a few of those), try this one: What two states share the distinction of having the lowest all-time high temperature. I bet you'll get one—Alaska—right off the bat. The second is the zinger—it's Hawaii. That's right, the temperature has never climbed above 100 degrees in the Aloha state, while

The highest year-round average temperature in the continental United States is the 78 degrees recorded in Key West, Florida, the southernmost point in the contiguous 48 states.

the thermometer has reached as high as 114 degrees in Minnesota and 121 degrees in North Dakota. If you hate hot weather and don't want to leave the continental United States, consider a move to Eureka, California—it's never been warmer than 85 degrees.

Anyone could guess that Hawaii is the one state in which the temperature has never gone below zero—the state record low is 14 degrees, recorded at the top of a 10,000-foot volcanic peak.

The all-time high and low temperatures for each state are:

	Record High	Record Low
Alabama	112	-24
Alaska	100	-80
Arizona	127	-40
California	134	-45
Colorado	118	-60
Connecticut	105	-32
Delaware	110	-17
Florida	109	-2
Georgia	112	-17
Hawaii	100	14
Idaho	118	-60
Illinois	117	-35
Indiana	116	-35
Iowa	118	-47
Kansas	121	-40
Kentucky	114	-34
Louisiana	114	-16
Maine	105	-48
Maryland	109	-40
Massachusetts	106	-34
Michigan	112	-51
Minnesota	114	-59
Mississippi	115	-19
Missouri	118	-40
Montana	117	-70
Nebraska	118	-47
Nevada	122	-50
New Hampshire	106	-46
New Jersey	110	-34
New Mexico	116	-50
New York	108	-52
North Carolina	109	-29
North Dakota	121	-60
Ohio	113	-39

Oklahoma	120	-27
Oregon	119	-54
Pennsylvania	111	-42
Rhode Island	102	-23
South Carolina	111	-13
South Dakota	120	-58
Tennessee	113	-32
Texas	120	-23
Utah	116	-50
Vermont	105	-50
Virginia	110	-29
Washington	118	-48
West Virginia	112	-37
Wisconsin	113	-54
Wyoming	114	-63

RECORD TEMPERATURE SWINGS

In the course of the average year, the range of temperatures recorded in the United States is often as great as 180 degrees—from temperatures as low as -60 degrees to as high as 120 degrees. What's really unusual is if the temperature spans a large chunk of that range in a matter of minutes.

If you think you have trouble deciding how to dress when the weather is changing, imagine yourself in front of the closet in Spearfish, South Dakota, on January 22, 1943. At 7:30 in the morning, the temperature climbed 49 degrees in just two minutes—from -4 degrees to 45 degrees. The temperature eventually reached 54 degrees by 9 A.M.—then a cold front swept back in and the temperature plummeted 58 degrees (back down to -4 degrees) in just 27 minutes.

The cause of this abrupt change was a warm Chinook wind roaring down the eastern slopes of the Rocky Mountains. Another Chinook raised the temperature 83 degrees, from -33 degrees to 50 degrees, over the course of 12 hours on February 21, 1918, in Granville, North Dakota. Yet a third warm wind melted 30 inches of snow as the temperature rose 80 degrees on December 1, 1896, in Kipp, Montana.

Rapid swings from warm to cold temperatures also occur in the winter months, when an Arctic cold front sweeps in to replace unusually warm air. The U.S. records are:

24 hours 100 degrees, from 44 degrees to -56 degrees, in Browning, Montana, on January 23, 1916

12 hours 84 degrees, from 63 degrees to -21 degrees, in Fairfield, Montana, on December 24, 1924

In the course of the average year, the range of temperatures recorded in the United States is often as great as 180 degrees.

2 hours 62 degrees, from 49 degrees to -13 degrees, in Rapid City, South Dakota, on January 12, 1911.

WHAT ARE THE "DOG DAYS"?

A spell of extremely hot weather, especially in August, is often referred to as the "dog days." This phrase doesn't come from pets panting in the heat. Rather, it dates all the way back to the ancient Egyptians, who believed that when Sirius, the Dog Star, rose with the sun, it added to the day's heat. So they considered the "dog days"—roughly July 3 to August 11—to be the hottest days of the year.

WHAT IS "INDIAN SUMMER"?

"Indian summer" is a uniquely American term for a period of unusually warm, calm, hazy weather that follows the first frost, usually in late October or early November. The term was first used after the American Revolution. Some writers, including the poet Henry Wadsworth Longfellow in his "Song of Hiawatha," traced the term to the Indian belief that the warm, hazy air result-ed when a powerful god had a last smoke of his pipe before sleep-ing through the winter. Other writers have mentioned another Indian legend that the gods send a warm, gentle breeze so prepa-rations for winter can be completed.

WHAT TEMPERATURE EXTREMES CAN THE HUMAN BODY STAND?

How much heat can the human body stand? In controlled exper-iments, subjects have tolerated temperatures in excess of 250 degrees for 15 minutes—with plenty to drink. In temperatures typical of Death Valley, a human being can become severely dehy-drated in a matter of minutes. The result is a rise in body temper-ature. Although there are unverified reports of people surviving body temperatures in excess of 120 degrees, temperatures in excess of 108 degrees are usually fatal.

There is evidence that human beings retain some kind of "hiber-nation reflex" that shuts down body functions and allows survival after short-term exposure to very cold temperatures. This reflex is strongest in children—there are many documented cases of chil-dren who have been submerged in freezing temperatures for 30 minutes or more and have survived.

Adults seldom survive if their body temperature drops below 85 degrees. However, in February 1951, a Chicago woman brought to the hospital for treatment for exposure had a body temperature of 64.5 degrees. Although her legs had to be amputated below the knee, she survived without brain damage.

RECORD PRECIPITATION

The rain in Spain may fall mainly on the plain (don't complain—it's a catchy refrain). But the heaviest year-round precipitation falls on the upslopes of tall mountain ranges. The all-time yearly precipitation record is an incredible 1,042 inches (that's almost 3 inches per day), which fell on Cherrapunji, India. Cherrapunji sits in the foothills of the mighty Himalayas, and for six months each year it is drenched as moisture-laden monsoon clouds slam into the mountain range.

In terms of average annual rainfall over decades, Cherrapunji (at 450 inches per year) is edged out for the title by Mt. Waialeale, on the Hawaiian Island of Kauai (at 460 inches per year). The U.S. all-time yearly precipitation record, 739 inches, is held by Kukui, on the Hawaiian island of Maui.

Thunderstorms and tropical storms normally account for the heaviest short-term rainfall totals. Following are some U.S. and world records:

1 minute (world)	1.5 inches	Guadeloupe, West Indies
1 minute (U.S.)	1.23 inches	Unionville, Maryland.
42 minutes (world)	12.00 inches	Holt, Missouri
2 hours, 45 minutes (world)	22.00 inches	D'Harris, Texas
12 hours (world)	45.00 inches	La Reunion (an island in the Indian Ocean near Madagascar)
12 hours (U.S.)	42.00 inches	Alvin, Texas
24 hours (world)	72.00 inches	La Reunion

At the other extreme is Arica, in Chile's Atacama Desert, which is in the rain shadow of the Andes Mountains. Average rainfall in Arica is just .03 of an inch per year, and the area has gone as long as 14 years without a drop falling. The other two areas in the world that average less than 1 inch of precipitation per year are Wadi Halfa, Sudan (in the Sahara Desert), and the South Pole, where the air is too cold to hold moisture.

The longest recorded period without rainfall in the United States was 767 days, from October 3, 1912, to November 8, 1914, in Bagdad, California. Death Valley, with a yearly average 1.63 inches of precipitation, is the driest location in the United States.

The longest recorded period without rainfall in the United States was 767 days, from October 3, 1912, to November 8, 1914, in Bagdad, California.

The driest states are all in the Southwest, the wettest in the Southeast. Except for the states of Washington and Oregon, precipitation averages rise as you move from west to east. Following is a list of states by average annual rainfall.

Under 10 inches

Nevada

10 to 19 inches

Alaska
Arizona
Colorado
Idaho
Montana
New Mexico
North Dakota
South Dakota
Utah
Wyoming

20 to 29 inches

California
Kansas
Minnesota
Nebraska
Oregon
Texas

30 to 39 inches

Hawaii
Illinois
Indiana
Iowa
Missouri

New York
Ohio
Oklahoma
Vermont
Washington
Wisconsin

40 to 49 inches

Arkansas
Connecticut
Delaware
Kentucky
Maine
Maryland
Massachusetts
New Hampshire
New Jersey
North Carolina
Pennsylvania
Rhode Island
South Carolina
Virginia
West Virginia

50 inches or more

Alabama
Florida
Georgia
Louisiana
Mississippi
Tennessee

High mountain areas of the American West hold all the U.S. snowfall records. They are:

24 hours	76 inches	Silver Lake, Colorado
1 storm	189 inches	Mt. Shasta Ski Bowl, California
1 season	1,122 inches	Paradise Ranger Station, Washington

Outside of the western mountains, the highest average annual snowfalls are recorded in northern Michigan, Upstate New York, and northern New England. Bennetts Bridge, New York, about 30 miles east of Oswego, may have experienced the greatest non-mountain snowfall on January 17, 1959, when 51 inches fell in 16 hours. Among the leaders in annual average are:

Marquette, Michigan	126.0 inches
Sault Ste. Marie, Michigan	116.4 inches
Caribou, Maine	113.3 inches
Syracuse, New York	110.5 inches

The line between the part of the country in which snow is a regular part of winter weather (an average of 12 inches per year or more) and the part of the country in which snow is infrequent runs roughly from Washington, D.C., across the northern borders of North Carolina, Tennessee, Arkansas, Oklahoma, and Texas to the southern border of the Rocky Mountains.

FLOODS

Although powerful hurricanes like 1992's Andrew can cause catastrophic damage, floods cost Americans more money year in and year out than do any other natural disaster. Floods are also the leading cause of weather-related deaths, killing an average of 113 people per year over the last decade.

The most famous and most deadly flood in U.S. history occured in Johnstown, Pennsylvania, on May 31, 1889, and killed 2,200 people. The most recent major flood disaster (July 31, 1976) was a flash flood in Big Thompson Canyon, 50 miles of northwest of Denver, Colorado, which killed 139 people.

Flooding caused by 100-mile-per-hour typhoon winds may have produced the greatest weather-related disaster in recorded history, in Bangladesh on November 13, 1970. Tides 10 to 15 feet above normal flooded 1.1 million acres. More than 1 million animals were drowned, and human deaths, first reported at 500,000, may also have exceeded 1 million people.

STRANGE PRECIPITATION

Since long before biblical times, literature is filled with reports of strange objects falling from the heavens. Many of these reports have a basis in fact.

The Bible talks about "manna" falling from heaven. This manna may actually have been a lichen that sprouts profusely after heavy rains, as if it fell from above.

"Rains of blood" are also relatively common. The red coloring comes from either desert dust or red algae carried into the clouds

The most famous and most deadly flood in U.S. history occured in Johnstown, Pennsylvania, on May 31, 1889, and killed 2,200 people.

by whirlwinds. In northern Europe, desert dust blown across the Mediterranean from the Sahara sometimes produces red snowfalls.

Over the last two decades, more than 100 rains of frogs, fish, eels, black worms, snakes, freshwater mussels, grasshoppers, locusts, and other living things have been reported. These creatures have either been sucked up by whirlpools (in the case of aquatic animals) or blown up into the air by the winds (in the case of insects).

However, no one's ever observed it literally "raining cats and dogs." So where does this phrase come from? One explanation is that it derives from Norse mythology, in which the cat is identified with strong storms and the dog with winds. So "raining cats and dogs" would mean heavy downpours with gusty winds. Another school holds that the phrase is a corruption of the Latin term "cata doxas," which means "contrary to experience." So "raining cata doxas [or cats and dogs]" means unusually heavy rain.

POWERFUL WINDS

The use of the figure of a cock to adorn the vanes was mandated by a papal decree in the ninth century.

There's one official weather record that everyone agrees has assuredly been surpassed: a wind speed of 231 miles per hour atop New Hampshire's Mount Washington. Even though that was an incredible gale, scientists have estimated winds inside tornadoes have reached 300 miles per hour or more—but they can't prove it, because no recording instrument has ever survived such a storm. Meteorologists also suspect that higher wind speeds have occurred over the oceans of the southern hemisphere and Antarctica—but there are no recording stations in those remote areas to measure them.

We do know that Mount Washington, with winds that average 35 miles per hour year around, is by far the windiest spot in the United States. Many locations in Alaska have significantly higher average wind speeds than do any cities in the lower 48 states. But average annual wind speed can be a very deceiving statistic. For instance, the mean wind speed in Chicago, the "Windy City," is less than one mile per hour less than the mean wind speed in New York. Chicago earned its moniker because it is occasionally forced to endure gale-force winds blowing unimpeded from the vast plains of Canada. New York, a coastal city, experiences measurable but more moderate breezes many more days per year.

WHY ARE COCKS PORTRAYED ON WEATHER VANES?

The use of weather vanes to show wind direction (remember, the arrow points toward the direction from which the wind is blowing) dates back to ancient times. The use of the figure of a cock to adorn the vanes was mandated by a papal decree in the ninth century. The symbolism: St. Peter denied Christ three times before the cock crowed twice. The purpose of the symbol: to remind the populace how vulnerable they were to temptation. Long after the decree was forgotten, the custom remained.

ARE WOOLLY BEARS WEATHER-WISE?: A GUIDE TO FACT AND FOLKLORE

21

After two decades as a weatherman, I've developed a pretty thick skin. But I have to confess that it still bugs me every time I'm asked, "How come a woolly bear knows when the winter will be harsh and you don't?" What they're really saying is, "Spencer, how come you're dumber than an insect?" I'm tempted to reply, "If you think woolly bears are so smart, why don't you let one do your tax return? Or be your Trivial Pursuit partner?" Of course, I'm too polite to say these things.

The truth is, though, that woolly bears aren't smarter than meteorologists (though they may be cuter). The width of the stripes on these caterpillars' backs (folklore says that if the brown stripe is wider than the black stripes, the winter will be long and harsh) is determined by a combination of genetics and the environmental conditions when the insect is growing. Scientific studies have shown absolutely no correlation between the width of the stripes and future weather.

But laying the woolly bear myth to bed doesn't mean that you and I should dismiss all weather sayings and folklore. As I have mentioned previously, in the thousands of years before the development of sophisticated instruments and supercomputers, humans had to depend on their keen powers of observation for clues to the upcoming weather. These observations produced many nuggets of wisdom that are still useful to us today.

Of course, along with the wisdom is a lot of superstition. I have always found separating fact from folklore to be a fascinating activity. I think you'll enjoy discovering which weather sayings have some basis in truth and which are fiction.

ANIMALS

- Swallows fly high, clear blue sky
  Swallows fly low, rain we shall know.

- Fish bite just before it rains.

- Before a storm, cows will lie down and refuse to go out to pasture.

- Cats will lick themselves constantly before a storm.

- It will be a cold, snowy winter if:

   - Squirrels accumulate huge stores of nuts.
   - Beavers build heavier lodges than usual.
   - Hair on bears and horses is thick early in season.
   - The breastbone of a fresh-cooked turkey is dark purple.

Falling air pressure may affect the digestive systems of cows, making them less willing to go to pasture.

Many ancient peoples worshiped animals, and an extension of that worship was the belief that certain animals had the ability to predict the future. Although such prognostication techniques as examining the entrails of a goat have been long abandoned (except for really important occasions such as our "Good Morning America" planning sessions), many people still accept the idea that animals are somehow "smarter" about nature than we are. That's why weather sayings and folklore involving animals are so prevalent.

Which of these beliefs are true? To understand, compare some fish, animals, and birds to weather instruments such as barometers, thermometers, hygrometers, and weather vanes. Because most species are very vulnerable to environmental changes, they may be sensitive to slight changes in air pressure, humidity, temperature, and wind direction that we humans can't detect. For example, swallows flying unusually low indicate that the air pressure is dropping, in the same way that the level of mercury in a barometer falls. Because a drop in air pressure can be a sign of approaching inclement weather, low-flying swallows are a sign that the chance of rain has increased.

Falling air pressure may affect the digestive systems of cows, making them less willing to go to pasture. Static electricity in the air before a storm may increase the grooming activities of cats. When seagulls stay close to shore, so do fishermen, who have noticed that such avian behavior often precedes storms. The cawing of crows, the honking of geese and the calls of other birds become louder and more frequent as low-pressure areas approach. There's evidence that deer and elk react to wind and air pressure changes by coming down from mountains and seeking shelter. Many species from rabbits to rattlesnakes to certain kinds of fish may feed more frenetically before a storm, during which they seek shelter.

I want to emphasize that these creatures are not making weather predictions; they are simply reacting to existing environmental conditions. If you're interested in what the weather will be like in three months, you'll have about the same luck asking your thermometer as you would checking out the food supply in a squirrel's nest or the size of a beaver's lodge. A bear or a horse may grow a heavier coat if November is especially cold, but that doesn't necessarily mean the entire winter will be harsh—December 1989 was the fourth-coldest December in U.S. history, while January 1990 was the warmest in history. If you're interested in finding out if squirrels or horses have any psychic power to predict the weather, you'll have to consult your Oujda board.

Topping the list of most bizarre animal folklore is the belief that the tissue of animals retains the ability to predict weather long after the creature's death. The Apache Indians believed that certain patterns that formed in bear fat were signs of certain types of approaching weather. I think getting a bear to cooperate is just the first of many problems with this forecasting theory.

INSECTS, WORMS, AND OTHER CREEPY, CRAWLY THINGS

- You can find out the temperature by counting the number of times a cricket chirps in 15 seconds and adding 40.

- When spiders weave their webs by noon, Fine weather is coming soon.

- Flies and gnats swarm and bite before a storm.

- If wasps build their nests high, the winter will be long and harsh.

In 1851, Dr. George Merryweather (with whom I feel a kinship, since I'm a merry weatherman) arrived at London's Great Exhibition with his revolutionary new weather-predicting invention, which consisted of 12 leeches, 12 jars, and a bell. When the leeches became active, they would trip a switch that rang a bell that warned of an approaching storm. Merryweather urged the British government to established a network of leech-activated bells along the entire length of that country's coastline.

The good doctor's suggestion wasn't implemented, but he also wasn't laughed out of town. For hundreds of years, people had related leech activity to the arrival of foul weather—with some justification. Insects, as well as other animals, are extremely sensitive to changes in their environments. When the air pressure drops, flying insects from flies to mosquitoes are much more active and stay closer to the ground. Cicadas hum loudly in dry weather, but can't vibrate their wings when the humidity is very high. Bees have difficulty carrying pollen when the humidity is very high, which makes them buzz irritably. A number of scientific studies have shown that the frequency of cricket chirps is directly related to temperature (if you're interested in the temperature at cricket-level).

But even though we weatherpeople may bug you, you can't turn instead to any insect for long-range forecasts, whether it's a wasp or a woolly bear.

PLANTS

- Seaweed dry, sunny sky;
  Seaweed wet, rain you'll get.

- When leaves show their undersides,
  Be very sure that rain betides.

- Dandelions close up before a storm.

- If onion skins are very thin,
  Then winter's mild when coming in
  But if onion skins are thick and tough,
  Then winter's long, cold, and rough.

- If oak is out before the ash,
  'Twill be a summer of wet and splash.
  But if the ash is before the oak,
  'Twill be a summer of fire and smoke.

We all know that plants are very sensitive to climate (for example, I wouldn't advise investing in a banana plantation in Minnesota). So it isn't strange that some respond visibly to subtle changes in the weather, especially changes in humidity. Seaweed and moss absorb moisture easily. A number of flowers, such as the scarlet pimpernel, tulips, African marigolds, and clover, close up as the humidity rises so that rain doesn't wash away their pollen. The leaves of many trees curl just before a storm, exposing their undersides.

But plant characteristics that supposedly predict future weather have a lot more to do with the weather that has already occurred. For example, a thick onion skin results from a dry summer—it doesn't mean that the onion knows that the upcoming winter will be harsh (where is an onion's brain, anyway?). Specific combinations of temperature and moisture determine whether an oak tree or an ash tree buds first—again, the trees don't "know" what the summer's weather will be like.

THE SKY AND THE CLOUDS

- Red sky at night, sailors' delight;
  Red sky in morning, sailors take warning.

- Mare's tails and mackeral scales,
  Make lofty ships carry low sails.

- When clouds appear like rocks and towers,
  The earth's refreshed with frequent showers.

- A halo around the moon,
  Means rain soon.

- Rainbow in the eastern sky,
  The morrow will be dry;
  Rainbow in the west that gleams,
  Rain falls in streams.

Of all weather sayings, the oldest and the most reliable are those that involve observation of the sky and the clouds. For example, read the following bits of wisdom about the meaning of red skies at sunset and sunrise:

When it is evening you say, "It will be fair weather, for the sky is red." And in the morning, "It will be stormy today, for the sky is red and threatening."

Matthew 16:2

A red morn, that ever yet betokened
Wreck to the seaman, tempest to the field,
Sorrow to the shepherds, woe unto the birds,
Gust and foul flaws to the herdsman and herds.

Shakespeare, *The Tempest*

The facts behind this folklore rest on the principle that weather basically moves from west to east. In order for the sun to reflect from clouds, the western horizon must be clear, which means fair skies will probably move in. On the other hand, a red sunrise means that sunlight is reflecting from high clouds moving in from the west, clouds that are often forerunners of storm systems.

Rainbows are produced by the refraction of light by rain. If you see a rainbow in the west, the rain is headed your way; a rainbow in the east means the weather system has passed.

Another common forerunner of precipitation is the presence of moisture (in the form of ice crystals) in the upper atmosphere. These crystals refract light, producing a "halo" around the sun or the moon. These ice crystals can produce high cirrus clouds that clump together. At night, these clumps block parts of the sky, so that the remaining stars seem to "huddle" together. Hence the saying, "When stars huddle, we'll be stepping in puddles."

Finally, as I mentioned in my discussion of skywatching, the shape and movement of clouds is often an accurate indication of weather to come.

WIND

- When the wind is in the north,
  The skillful fisher goes not forth;
  When the wind is in the east,
  'Tis good for neither man nor beast;
  When the wind is in the south,
  It blows the flies in the fish's mouth;
  But when the wind is in the west,
  There it is the very best.

- A veering wind will clear the sky,
  A backing wind says storms are nigh.

Observations about the wind and wind shifts are as ancient and as generally reliable as observations of the sky and clouds. For example, mariners have long taken note of the changes in wind direction when high- and low-pressure systems approach. Because winds circulate in a clockwise direction around a high, wind direction will shift from southwest to west to northwest. This pattern is called a "veering wind" and is a sign of approaching fair weather. Because winds circulate in a counterclockwise direction around a low, wind direction will shift from northeast to north to northwest. This pattern is a called a "backing wind" and is a sign of approaching inclement weather.

Wind direction is also a good indication of local weather. In the northern hemisphere, an east wind often brings bad weather, as described in the Bible:

God prepared a vehement east wind.—*Jonah 4:8*

Thou breakest the ships of Tarish with an east wind.—*Psalms 48:7*

The settlers in the New World also found an east world threatening:

When the wind is from the east
Neither good for man nor beast.

Numerous popular sayings point out that a south wind brings rain, a west wind fair weather, and a north wind bitter cold.

USING OUR SENSES

- The squeak of the snow will the temperature show.

- Ditches and manure piles smell stronger just before it rains.

- Sound travels far and wide, a stormy day will betide.

- The farther the sight, the nearer the rain.

- Some people feel rain in their bones.

Even though computers now generate the raw materials of our weather forecasts, there was a much longer time in human history when we were as dependent on intepreting subtle changes in our environment as animals and insects are today. We don't squawk when the pressure drops or curl up when it's humid, but we can learn to use our senses to recognize potential weather changes.

One clue is sound. Generally, the higher the humidity, the better sound travels. In some English cities, citizens gauged the chances of rain by the clarity with which they heard church bells sound. The sound of our footsteps on snow also provides an indication of the temperature—the louder the squeak, the colder the air.

The common saying is true: We can "smell" rain, even though water vapor has no odor. How? Well, plants exude oils that are absorbed by the soil. When the air pressure drops, the soil releases some of these oils, producing a smell we've learned to interpret as the "smell of rain." Dropping air pressure also intensifies the odors of flowers and manure.

Since the beginning of recorded history, people have noted that faraway objects appear closer before a storm. The reason for this optical illusion is a difference in temperature between levels of air. Normally, the temperature drops about 1 degree Fahrenheit every 300 feet of elevation. If certain weather conditions cause the upper air to be warmer than normal, light is refracted differently, distorting this view. The result is a type of mirage called the Hillenger Effect.

Can you feel rain in your bones? If you have arthritis or rheumatism, you may well be able to. Numerous studies have found some correlation between a drop in barometric pressure and discomfort suffered by people with joint diseases, as well as those with bad teeth, recently healed broken bones, and corns and bunions.

Finally, the weather also seems to affect our moods. In particular, a combination of low barometric pressure and high humidity has been linked to an increase in suicide and criminal behavior. Some Native American tribes used this increased irritability to their advantage by planning battles as storms approached, hence the saying "Storm gods give courage to the red man."

CONTINUITY OF PATTERNS

• As many days old as is the moon on the day of the first snow, there will be that many snowfalls by crop planting time.

• The first frost in autumn will be exactly six months after the first thunderstorm of the spring.

• St. Swithin's Day, if it do rain,
  For forty days it will remain.

• If Candlemas Day be mild and gay,
  Go saddle your horses and buy them hay.
  If Candlemas Day be stormy and black,
  It carries the winter on its back.

Early man saw many regular patterns in nature: the rising and setting of the sun, the phases of the moon, the rhythmic movements of the tides. So it was natural to assume that the weather also fell into predictable patterns. Early folklore contains hundreds of sayings linking the phases of the moon, the appearance of the stars, and the occurrence of events such as the first frost to later weather events. It would be a terrific help to us weather forecasters if some were true—I'd just note the date of the first autumn frost, and my spring thunderstorm forecast would be ready! But, alas, nature isn't very cooperative when it comes to long-range forecasting.

The most persistent bit of folklore based on continuity of patterns is our Groundhog Day. The rather bizarre custom of lurking by a burrow on February 2 in hopes of finding out how long winter is going to last comes directly from a centuries-old English tradition involving Candlemas Day, the Catholic celebration of the feast of the purification of Mary. Farmers have believed for thousands of years that the month of February somehow "breeds" weather for the rest of the year. For some reason, the English decided that February 2 was the key day; if the weather was clear and fair, the winter would last six more weeks; if the weather was dark and stormy, winter was over.

Farmers have believed for thousands of years that the month of February somehow "breeds" weather for the rest of the year.

English settlers brought the tradition to the United States, and in our own inimitable fashion, we transferred the emphasis to a groundhog. The American tradition says that if the groundhog pops up on a sunny day, it will be so frightened by its shadow that it will dart back into the ground, bringing six more weeks of winter. On the other hand, if it emerges on a cloudy day and isn't frightened, it will stay out to romp, signaling winter's end.

THE PRINCIPLE OF COMPENSATION

- A severe summer denotes a windy autumn;
  A windy winter a rainy spring;
  A rainy spring a severe summer;
  A severe summer a windy autumn;
  So that the air in balance is
  Seldom debtor unto itself.

- A month that comes in good, goes out bad.

- A warm Christmas,
  A cold Easter.

Yet another ancient belief that has given rise to a large volume of weather folklore is that nature seeks a balance—for example, a warm summer means a cold winter; a dry spring means ample summer rainfall; a windy autumn is followed by a mild winter. You can't imagine how many times I have wished these bits of wisdom were true—I'd just tell every caller who complained about the bitterly cold winter, "I guarantee you'll enjoy a nice, warm, sunny spring." But once again, when it comes to long-term weather, Mother Nature has the world's best poker face—we just have to wait and see.

PEERING INTO THE CRYSTAL BALL: THE WEATHER AND OUR FUTURE

Despite all the recent talk about global warming and other dangers that threaten dramatic climate change, most of us find it very difficult to accept the idea that basic weather patterns where we live can be disrupted. The rhythms of nature have been and are an integral part of our lives; we grow accustomed to seeing spring flowers emerge at the same time each year, of watching perennials in our gardens bloom every summer, of timing events in our lives by the changing colors of leaves. It doesn't seem possible that our children and our children's children won't have the same experience.

Yet, at the same time, a growing body of evidence is bringing us to our senses. I was particularly struck by a recent archaeological discovery in the South of France. Three years ago, divers probing the Mediterranean coast found the submerged entrance to a cave. After swimming in about 500 yards, they found themselves surfacing in a huge vault covered with primitive paintings. Astonished scientists soon discovered that this art dated back to 20,000 B.C., 8,000 years further than other cave paintings found in Europe. And even more amazing than the date was the subject of many of the drawings: penguins. That's right, just 22,000 years ago, the beaches of the South of France, where tourists now bask in the warm Mediterranean sun year-round, were a playground for penguins sliding on the ice and snow before taking a dip in the frigid water.

That climate can change so dramatically in such a short span of time is a sobering thought. When you add mankind's newly acquired ability to affect our environment, the probability of change in the lifetime of our children and grandchildren quickly moves from inconceivable to possible. As a weather journalist, I have spent an enormous amount of time investigating the subject of climate change, and I want to share with you what I know and what I believe.

22

Just 22,000 years ago, the beaches of the South of France were a playground for penguins.

WHAT ARE THE NATURAL MECHANISMS
OF CLIMATE CHANGE?

Over the course of its history, the Earth has been so warm that vegetation flourished at the North Pole and so cold that vast glaciers have covered most of the middle latitudes. Although the science of climatology is in its infancy, we suspect that there are three major reasons for this temperature swing.

First, both the orbit of the Earth around the sun and the angle (or tilt) of the Earth's axis in relation to the sun changes. The time of year when the Earth is closest to the sun changes in a 23,000-year cycle—it's now closest in January, but in 10,000 years it will be closest in July. The tilt of the Earth's axis becomes more or less perpendicular in about a 40,000-year cycle. Finally, the Earth's orbit changes from nearly circular to more elliptical in a 93,000-year cycle. All of these changes affect climate.

Second, the sun's output varies in a cycle that ranges from a few decades to tens of thousands of years or more. Short-term variations in energy coming from our star have been linked to significant short-term global cooling. We are just beginning to investigate the range and significance of long-term variations.

Finally, the amount of dust in the atmosphere varies over the course of years and decades. This dust absorbs solar energy that would otherwise reach the ground, causing cooler temperatures. For most of Earth's history, volcanic activity has been the primary cause of this dust. Today, pollutants generated by our technology may eventually have a similar effect.

The sun's output varies in a cycle that ranges from a few decades to tens of thousands of years or more.

IF WE WEREN'T SPEWING STUFF INTO THE AIR,
WHAT NATURAL CLIMATE CHANGES
COULD WE EXPECT?

If I had a definitive answer to that, I'd be a Nobel laureate. I do know that for most of the last billion years, global temperatures have been significantly warmer than they are today. On the other hand, several ice ages have occurred over the last million years, with the effects of the last one (as evidenced by our Mediterranean penguins) lingering until at least 22,000 years ago. So the Earth could either cool off to the point at which another ice age begins, or it could warm to temperature levels more characteristic of the last billion years.

One reason that we just don't know what to expect is that these natural climate changes take place slowly. Mankind would have hundreds, perhaps thousands, of years to adapt. While some adaptations might be expensive and difficult, the human race—given our technical ingenuity—would in all probability survive.

WHY ARE MANMADE CLIMATE CHANGES SO POTENTIALLY DANGEROUS?

Over the last two years, we have all emerged from the shadow of nuclear war, a cataclysmic event that would in 24 hours drastically alter (and perhaps end) human life. But we may in fact be unknowingly creating conditions that may drastically alter our climate over a timespan of one or two hundred years—a timeframe so short that the effects might be nearly as cataclysmic as nuclear war. Although our crystal ball is as murky as the air over Los Angeles, the two most pressing dangers seem to be global warming produced by carbon dioxide emission and destruction of the Earth's ozone layer.

WHAT IS GLOBAL WARMING?

Global warming is the phrase most commonly used to indicate the end result of the accumulation in the air of certain gases that would increase the "greenhouse effect" provided by the Earth's atmosphere. In plain language, here's how it works. If the Earth had no atmosphere, it would radiate back into space about the same amount of energy it receives from the sun. That would mean global temperatures would average about 0 degrees Fahrenheit. Fortunately, some substances in the air, primarily water vapor and carbon dioxide, intercept the escaping energy and radiate it back toward Earth—just as the dome of a greenhouse traps heat. As a result, global temperatures average about 59 degrees Fahrenheit.

We don't hear much about water vapor and the greenhouse effect because humans don't have much to do with the water cycle. However, since the middle of the 19th century, we have been burning an increasing amount of fossil fuels. One result of this combustion is a tremendous increase in carbon dioxide emitted into the air, and about half of this excess gas accumulates in the atmosphere. The accumulation rate could be even higher if more of the Earth's forest areas (trees absorb carbon dioxide) are destroyed. Some scientists estimate that the amount of atmospheric carbon dioxide could double in the next 75 years. This gas, along with an increase in other greenhouse gases, such as methane (produced by the fermentation in the stomachs of cows and other livestock) and nitrous oxide, could increase global temperatures by as much as 7 degrees Fahrenheit.

WHAT WOULD BE THE RESULTS OF GLOBAL WARMING?

I'm going to answer this question as I have so many in this chapter: We don't know for sure. Many scientists believe that the Arctic ice cap would begin to melt, raising sea levels by as much as seven inches. This increase would drown many of the major sea-coast cities in the world. At the other pole, the ice cap over Antarctica may grow, because increased water vapor in the air would increase snowfall over the southernmost continent.

With the Arctic ice cap shrinking, the arena in which warm and cold air clashes would move farther north. Vast regions of Canada could become fertile farm areas, while higher temperatures and lower precipitation levels turn now-fertile areas of the United States into semi-arid regions. At the other extreme, the lower contrast between warm- and cold-water regions could weaken or eliminate the Gulf Stream. The British Isles and Western Europe, now warmed by the Gulf Stream, could experience sharply colder weather.

Although they may not agree on the consequences of global warming, scientists are nearly unanimous in their concern that any kind of rapid climate change could prove catastrophic on a regional or even global scale. We know too little about the extremely complex workings of our global climate to be able to tinker with it with confidence.

Any kind of rapid climate change could prove catastrophic on a regional or even global scale.

WHAT CAN WE DO ABOUT GLOBAL WARMING?

Our world is so dependent on fossil fuels that drastic action is impossible. Over the long term, we will eventually run out of fossil fuels. So the faster we convert to alternative energy sources—solar, nuclear, wind—the better. In the meantime, energy conservation and efforts to limit pollution are our practical options.

However, these options will not prevent a dramatic increase in greenhouse gases. Our best hope of surviving dramatic warming is to increase our knowledge of the global weather machine so we can better predict—and thus prepare for—whatever changes that global warming, if any, will bring.

THE DANGER OF OZONE DESTRUCTION

Without the whisper thin protective layer high in the stratosphere, the sun's ultra-violet rays could make the surface of the Earth as inhospitable to life as some alien planet.

Fortunately, we know exactly what causes ozone destruction—the chlorine in chorofluorocarbons (CFCs), very useful substances used as, among other things, refrigerants, solvents, and components of foam. Protecting the ozone requires a total ban on CFCs. Because of the economic and practical hardships involved in such a ban, governments have been dragging their feet. Although balancing economic concerns with environmental concerns is difficult in many areas, it's hard for me to understand how anyone could believe that the scale tilts toward short-term financial gain rather than toward preventing the destruction of life on Earth.

WILL WE EVER BE ABLE TO MAKE POSITIVE CHANGES IN OUR CLIMATE?

Over the last few decades, various experiments in changing the weather have been conducted in several parts of the world, experiments that point out that the obvious benefits of weather modification may be outweighed by equal, or greater, liabilities. For example, the U.S. government tried to weaken hurricanes by seeding clouds. While there is some evidence that these efforts had a small, temporary effect, some Caribbean nations threatened legal action, claiming that disrupting the normal path of tropical weather systems would deprive them of vital rainfall. The experiments have now been suspended.

The terrible damage caused by some tornadoes has led some to call for experiments designed to prevent the formation of supercell thunderstorms. But thunderstorms provide up to 75 percent of the annual yearly precipitation in some central United States. How do we balance saving 100 lives a year against turning the region into a dust bowl?

Climate modification may be in mankind's future. But before that future arrives, there has to be a vast increase in our knowledge of the way our global climate works.

UNFORESEEN CATASTROPHES

The universe is a dangerous, even hostile place. Over the last 3 billion years, three or four catastrophic events—probably impacts of giant asteroids—have come close to wiping out all life on Earth. Although the chances of another such event occurring in our lifetimes are infinitesimal (much less than the chances of being struck by lightning), it is a virtual certainty that another such event (or several) will occur before our sun burns out 5 billion years from now. Even when we develop the ability to detect dangerous asteroids heading toward us and to launch a missile to destroy them, some other now-unforeseen calamity will pose an equal threat. Although speculating on what that danger could be is a fascinating exercise, it has little practical value now.

SO WHAT EXACTLY DO YOU SEE IN YOUR CRYSTAL BALL, SPENCER?

The world's leading scientists and I have about the same chance of making accurate predictions about the weather five, 10, 20, or 100 years from now as we would predicting who will win the Super Bowl in the year 2000.

What I can accurately predict, however, is that our new environmental awareness and concern will continue to grow throughout this decade. All of us are beginning to realize that weather means far more than whether or not we need an umbrella tomorrow. Global climate has a profound effect on our economic, political, social, and cultural future. Worries about mankind's impact on our climate are not just the obsession of a few fanatics, but legitimate concerns for any reasonable citizen.

All of us, from scientists to elementary school students, need to increase our knowledge of the ways in which our protective atmospheric blanket works. Such knowledge will allow us to make increasingly intelligent decisions about our lifestyles and our voting choices.

As a journalist, I have a challenging and exciting task ahead of me—monitoring the latest discoveries, most recent problems and proposed solutions, then explaining them to you. I promise to do my best to prepare you not just for the weather tomorrow, but for the environmental challenges of the 21st century. I hope you'll be watching (and reading).

HOW TO BECOME A WEATHER WATCHER

23

Way back in the Introduction to this book, I admitted that I wasn't particularly fascinated by the weather while I was growing up. What I failed to add was that over the last two decades, watching the weather has not only become my vocation, but an avocation of mine as well. One of the reasons I love to travel is that I look forward to learning about local weather conditions and hearing stories of bizarre weather events. The factors that create our weather and global climate are so intricate, so complicated, that any of us could spend several lifetimes of study and still not solve all the mysteries.

My enthusiasm is shared by a huge group of weather hobbyists all over the country. Some serve as official observers for the U.S. Weather Service. Many more make the job of my colleagues on local newscasts much easier by serving as volunteer "weather watchers." And nearly everyone I've talked with who has begun observing and recording weather conditions on a regular basis considers the experience richly rewarding.

I hope that reading this book has made you more interested in your local weather and climate. If it has, the tips below will allow you to become a thoroughly professional amateur weather observer.

One of the best things about being a weather watcher is that weather happens every day, and it happens right in your backyard.

THE WHERE AND WHEN OF WEATHER WATCHING

One of the best things about being a weather watcher is that weather happens every day, and it happens right in your backyard. To get an accurate picture of your climate, you have to make weather observations every day—preferably twice per day. The U.S. Weather Service makes its official observations every day at noon and midnight Greenwich Mean Time, which means 7 A.M. and 7 P.M. Eastern Standard Time, 6 A.M. and 6 P.M. Central, 5 A.M. and 5 P.M. Mountain, and 4 A.M. and 4 P.M. Pacific. If you record your observations at the same time, you can compare them with the official readings listed in your local newspaper and reported on TV. However, your convenience is the most important factor—pick times when you (or a family member) are likely to be available every day.

WHAT INSTRUMENTS DO YOU NEED
AND WHERE DO YOU PUT THEM?

Meteorology doesn't have to be an expensive hobby. You can begin with some very inexpensive equipment and gradually add to your weather kit over a few years.

The following is a list of the basics and what you'd like to have to be "fully equipped":

• Measuring temperature. The Fahrenheit scale is used by the U.S. Weather Service for surface observations; an outdoor Fahrenheit thermometer is extremely inexpensive. I recommend spending a few extra cents for one that is calibrated in both the Fahrenheit and Celsius scales.

High on your wish list should be a thermometer that records the maximum and minimum temperatures over a given period. The most common design dates back over 200 years; the most modern are digital thermometers with built-in memory. Either one will allow you to record the daily high and low temperatures at your location and compare them with the official U.S. Weather Service readings for your area.

Any thermometer that you purchase should be mounted out-doors in a grassy area—any hard surface will radiate heat that renders your readings inaccurate. The thermometer should also be protected from direct sunlight and the harshest wind and rain. Official weather observers put their thermometers in a box with a top and louvered sides so air can flow freely.

• Measuring rain and snow. To start, you can make a rain gauge for my favorite dollar amount: $0.00. Just set up a tall round glass or a metal can with straight sides in an exposed spot, then use a ruler to measure any accumulation when you take your twice daily observations. Empty the gauge after each reading.

You can upgrade inexpensively by purchasing one of the several models of plastic rain gauges sold in garden centers or hardware stores. These are easy to mount and are already calibrated. They are easier to read than a homemade gauge, but they are not signif-icantly more accurate.

For accuracy matching that of the Weather Service, you need the type of gauge I described earlier in this book: an instrument with a wide mouth that funnels rain into a tube exactly one-tenth the diameter. If you're handy, you can check out the fancy versions in a science store, then see if you can make your own.

Measuring snowfall accurately is extremely difficult, even for professionals. Using a ruler to measure depth of snow in a number of open spots will give you a good-enough idea of how much snow has fallen. You can leave measuring the water content of snow to the professionals.

• Measuring atmospheric pressure. Reading the barometer is my favorite weather job—because air pressure is the same indoors and outdoors, I set mine up where I can glance over from my easy chair. Because indoor barometers are decorative as well as functional, they vary widely in price—but you don't have to spend a lot for a "plain vanilla" instrument that will give accurate readings.

Whatever barometer you used will have to be adjusted for your height above sea level. The best way to do this is to call your local Weather Service office for an official reading, and set yours to the same measure. Then set up the barometer out of the sunlight in a place with relatively constant temperature.

• Measuring wind speed and direction. All you need to record wind direction is a wind sock or wind vane and a small compass. You can make your own wind sock, or you can purchase one at a garden or hardware store. Record wind direction by the eight points of the compass: north, northeast, east, southeast, etc. Remember: The wind is labeled by the direction it is blowing *from* (a northeast wind is blowing from northeast to southwest).

Many weather observers estimate wind speed by using the Beaufort scale, which I included in my chapter on wind. By comparing your estimates with the official U.S. Weather Service readings, you'll soon become quite accurate. If you really become serious about your hobby, you might eventually purchase an anemometer, which electronically records wind speed.

Some of your most valuable weather information will come from equipment you already have— your ears and eyes.

• Measuring humidity. Least expensive are hygrometers that use the expansion and contraction of human hair, paper, or some other substance to measure humidity. These instruments aren't very accurate, so I'd recommend saving your money and using official readings instead.

Eventually, you'd like to be able to take wet-bulb and dry-bulb readings. The most accurate device is called a sling psychrometer: You moisten a sock, slip it on the wet bulb thermometer, then whirl it around with the sling until the moisture evaporates. Using tables that come with the instrument, you can then compute the relative humidity and the dew point.

YOUR OBSERVATIONS

Some of your most valuable weather information will come from equipment you already have—your ears and eyes. Your observations are a critical part of your weather records.

Twice a day you should record:

- Conditions. Is it raining, snowing, foggy, partly sunny, etc.?

- Clouds. You should note:

    The amount of sky covered by clouds (on a scale of 1 to 10)
    The height of the clouds (e.g., low, medium, or high)
    Type of clouds (cirrus, cumulus, etc.)
    Direction the clouds are moving

You will also want to remember any significant weather events that occurred each day—a particularly violent thunderstorm, tornado warning, flash flood, etc.

YOUR WEATHER LOG

Now that you have your instruments in place and you know what observations you're going to make, you need to develop a system for recording the information. Since jotting figures on the back of old envelopes is frowned on in scientific circles, you should use a weather log.

Weather logs with preprinted columns are available in science supply stores and by mail. But a spiral-bound notebook or a ledger works just as well. You'll want to have the following headings:

- Temperature   A.M. reading
  P.M. reading
  High temperature
  Low temperature
  Mean temperature

- Precipitation   A.M. reading
  P.M. reading

- Air pressure   A.M. reading
  A.M. tendency (Did air pressure rise or fall?)
  P.M. reading
  P.M. tendency

- Wind   A.M. wind direction
  A.M. wind speed
  P.M. wind direction
  P.M. wind speed

- Humidity   A.M. relative humidity
  A.M. dew point

P.M. relative humidity

P.M. dew point

- Conditions   A.M. Conditions

                         P.M. Conditions

- Clouds   A.M. cover

                         A.M. ceiling

                         A.M. cloud types and direction

                         P.M. cover

                         P.M. ceiling

                         P.M. cloud types and direction

- Notes and other observations

SO, NOW I'VE GOT THIS INFORMATION— WHAT'S NEXT?

When you first start out, simply recording all this information is a big enough task. But as you become more adept, you'll want to turn to the real fun of being a weather watcher—making your own predictions. I recommend using a separate notebook for recording your predictions (no cheating!) and comparing them to the actual result. The elements of your forecasts will be the same as the ones in my forecast:

- Temperatures (high and low)

- Precipitation

- Sky conditions (cloudy, partly cloudy, etc.)

- Wind speeds and direction

You should also try your hand at forecasting severe weather, from thunderstorms to blizzards. If you're diligent with your daily observations, you'll be surprised how skilled you become.

WHERE TO GET ADDITIONAL INFORMATION

As you become more and more involved in observing and predicting the weather, you'll be seeking out sources of additional information. I recommend the following:

- Field guides. A picture is often worth a thousand words when it comes to cloud formations and other sky conditions. *The Audubon Society Field Guide to North American Weather* (Alfred

A. Knopf, 1991) contains 378 gorgeous color photographs with detailed captions that you'll find an informative delight.

• Weather publications. The U.S. government uses our tax dollars to collect a vast amount of weather information, and they partially return the favor by publishing a large number of inexpensive publications and maps. You can contact:

Superintendent of Documents
Government Printing Office
Washington, DC 20402
Ask for the catalog *U.S. Government Books* and subject indexes for "Meteorology" and "Maps and Atlases."

National Climatic Data Center
Federal Building
Ashville, NC 28801
Ask for a list of publications.

National Weather Service
Public Affairs Office
1325 East-West Highway
Silver Spring, MD 20910
Ask for a list of publications.

National Oceanic and Atmospheric Administration
Logistics Supply Center
1500 E. Bannister Road
Kansas City, MO 64131
Ask for a list of publications.

U.S. Geological Survey
Federal Center
Box 25286
Washington, DC 20090
Ask for a list of publications.

• Organizations. You can obtain a host of publications and services from the following organizations:

American Association of Weather Observers
401 Whitney Blvd.
Belvidere, IL 61008

American Meteorological Society
1701 K St., NW
Washington, DC 20006

- Magazines. By far the best weather magazine is:

Weatherwise
Heldref Publications
1319 18th St., NW
Washington, DC 20036

- Books, Software, Instruments, Etc.

American Weather Enterprises
P.O. Box 1383
Media, PA 19063
Ask for a catalog.

AVERAGE MONTHLY TEMPERATURES
FOR 100 U.S. CITIES (°F.)

	Jan.	Apr.	July	Oct.
Albany, NY	21.1	46.6	71.4	50.5
Albuquerque, NM	34.8	55.1	78.8	57.4
Anchorage, AK	13.0	35.4	58.1	34.6
Asheville, NC	36.8	55.7	73.2	56.0
Atlanta, GA	41.9	61.8	78.6	62.2
Atlantic City, NJ	31.8	51.0	74.4	56.5
Austin, TX	49.1	68.7	84.7	69.8
Baltimore, MD	32.7	54.0	76.8	58.9
Baton Rouge, LA	50.8	68.4	82.1	68.2
Billings, MT	20.9	44.6	72.3	49.3
Birmingham, AL	42.9	62.8	80.1	62.6
Bismark, ND	6.7	42.5	70.4	46.1
Boise, ID	29.9	48.6	74.6	51.9
Boston, MA	29.6	48.7	73.5	54.8
Bridgeport, CT	29.5	48.6	74.0	56.0
Buffalo, NY	23.5	45.4	70.7	51.5
Burlington, VT	16.6	42.7	69.6	47.9
Caribou, ME	10.7	37.3	65.1	43.1
Casper, WY	22.2	42.1	70.9	47.1
Charleston, SC	47.9	64.3	80.5	65.8
Charleston, WV	32.9	55.3	74.5	55.9
Charlotte, NC	40.5	60.3	78.5	60.7
Cheyenne, WY	26.1	41.8	68.9	47.5
Chicago, IL	21.4	48.8	73.0	53.5
Cleveland, OH	25.5	48.1	71.6	53.2
Columbia, SC	44.7	63.8	81.0	63.4
Columbus, OH	27.1	51.4	73.8	53.9
Concord, NH	19.1	44.1	69.5	48.3
Dallas-Ft. Worth, TX	44.0	65.9	86.3	67.9
Denver, CO	29.5	47.4	73.4	51.9
Des Moines, IA	18.6	50.5	76.3	54.2
Detroit, MI	23.4	47.3	71.9	51.9
Dodge City, KA	29.5	54.3	80.0	57.7
Duluth, MN	6.3	38.3	65.4	44.2
El Paso, TX	44.2	63.6	82.5	63.6
Fairbanks, AK	-12.7	30.2	61.5	25.1
Fargo, ND	4.3	42.1	70.6	46.3
Grand Junction, CO	25.5	51.7	78.9	54.9
Grand Rapids, MI	22.0	46.3	71.4	50.9
Hartford, CT	25.2	48.8	73.4	52.4
Helena, MT	18.1	42.3	67.9	45.1

Honolulu, HI	72.6	75.7	80.1	79.5
Houston, TX	51.4	68.7	83.1	69.7
Indianapolis, IN	26.0	52.4	75.1	54.8
Jackson, MS	45.7	65.1	81.9	65.0
Jacksonville, FL	53.2	67.7	81.3	69.5
Juneau, AK	21.8	39.1	55.7	41.8
Kansas City, MO	28.4	56.9	80.9	59.6
Knoxville, TN	38.2	59.6	77.6	59.5
Las Vegas, NV	44.5	63.5	90.2	67.5
Lexington, KY	31.5	55.1	75.9	56.8
Little Rock, AR	39.9	62.4	82.1	63.1
Long Beach, CA	55.2	60.9	72.8	67.5
Los Angeles, CA	56.0	59.5	69.0	66.3
Louisville, KY	32.5	56.6	77.6	57.7
Madison, WI	15.6	45.8	70.6	49.5
Memphis, TN	39.6	62.6	82.1	62.9
Miami, FL	67.1	75.3	82.5	77.9
Milwaukee, WI	18.7	44.6	70.5	50.9
Minneapolis, MN	11.2	46.0	73.1	49.6
Mobile, AL	50.8	68.0	82.2	68.5
Montgomery, AL	46.7	65.2	81.7	65.3
Mt. Washington, NH	5.1	22.4	48.7	30.5
Nashville, TN	37.1	59.7	79.4	60.2
Newark, NJ	31.2	52.1	76.8	57.2
New Orleans, LA	52.4	68.7	82.1	69.2
New York, NY	31.8	51.9	76.4	57.5
Norfolk, VA	39.9	58.2	78.4	61.3
Oklahoma City, OK	35.9	60.2	82.1	62.3
Olympia, WA	37.2	47.3	63.0	50.1
Omaha, NE	20.2	52.2	77.7	54.5
Philadelphia, PA	31.2	52.9	76.5	56.5
Phoenix, AZ	52.3	68.1	92.3	73.4
Pittsburgh, PA	26.7	50.1	72.0	52.5
Portland, ME	21.5	42.8	68.1	48.5
Portland, OR	38.9	50.4	67.7	54.3
Providence, RI	28.2	47.9	72.5	53.2
Raleigh, NC	39.6	59.4	77.7	59.7
Reno, NV	32.2	46.4	69.5	50.3
Richmond, VA	36.6	57.9	77.8	58.6
Russell, NM	41.4	61.9	81.4	61.7
St. Louis, MO	28.8	56.1	78.9	57.9
Sacramento, CA	45.3	58.2	75.6	63.9
Salt Lake City, UT	28.6	49.2	77.5	53.0
San Antonio, TX	50.4	69.6	84.6	70.2
San Diego, CA	56.8	61.2	70.3	67.5
San Francisco, CA	48.5	54.8	62.2	60.6

Savannah, GA	49.1	66.0	81.2	66.9
Seattle, WA	39.1	48.7	64.8	52.4
Sioux Falls, SD	12.4	46.4	74.0	49.4
Spokane, WA	25.7	45.8	69.7	47.5
Springfield, IL	24.6	53.3	76.5	56.0
Tampa, FL	59.8	71.5	82.1	74.4
Toledo, OH	23.1	47.8	71.8	51.7
Tucson, AZ	51.1	64.9	86.4	70.4
Tulsa, OK	35.2	61.0	83.2	62.6
Vero Beach, FL	61.9	71.7	81.1	75.2
Washington, DC	35.2	56.7	78.9	59.3
Wilmington, DE	31.2	52.4	76.0	56.3
Wichita, KA	29.6	56.3	81.4	59.1

AVERAGE ANNUAL PRECIPITATION FOR 100 U.S. CITIES

	Rainfall	Snowfall	
	Average Inches	Average Inches	Days w/Precip.
Albany, NY	35.74	65.5	134
Albuquerque, NM	8.12	10.6	59
Anchorage, AK	15.20	69.2	115
Asheville, NC	47.71	17.5	124
Atlanta, GA	48.61	1.9	115
Atlantic City, NJ	41.93	16.4	112
Austin, TX	31.50	.9	83
Baltimore, MD	41.84	1.8	113
Baton Rouge, LA	55.77	.1	108
Billings, MT	15.09	57.2	96
Birmingham, AL	54.52	1.3	117
Bismark, ND	15.36	40.3	96
Boise, ID	11.71	21.4	92
Boston, MA	43.81	41.8	127
Bridgeport, CT	41.56	26.0	117
Buffalo, NY	37.52	92.2	169
Burlington, VT	33.69	78.2	153
Caribou, ME	36.59	13.3	160
Casper, WY	11.43	80.5	95
Charleston, SC	51.59	.6	113
Charleston, WV	42.43	31.5	151
Charlotte, NC	43.16	6.1	111
Cheyenne, WY	13.31	54.1	98
Chicago, IL	33.34	40.3	127
Cleveland, OH	35.40	53.6	156
Columbia, SC	49.12	1.9	109
Columbus, OH	36.97	28.3	137
Concord, NH	36.53	64.5	125
Dallas-Ft. Worth, TX	29.46	3.1	78
Denver, CO	15.31	59.8	88
Des Moines, IA	30.83	34.7	107
Detroit, MI	30.97	40.4	133
Dodge City, KA	20.66	19.5	78
Duluth, MN	29.68	77.4	135
El Paso, TX	7.82	5.2	47
Fairbanks, AK	10.37	67.5	106
Fargo, ND	19.59	35.9	100
Grand Junction, CO	8.00	26.1	72
Grand Rapids, MI	34.35	72.4	143

Hartford, CT	44.39	50.0	127
Helena, MT	11.37	47.9	96
Honolulu, HI	23.47	0.0	100
Houston, TX	44.76	.4	105
Indianapolis, IN	39.12	23.1	125
Jackson, MS	52.82	1.2	109
Jacksonville, FL	52.76	.1	116
Juneau, AK	53.15	102.8	220
Kansas City, MO	29.27	20.0	98
Knoxville, TN.	47.29	12.3	127
Las Vegas, NV	4.19	1.4	26
Lexington, KY	45.68	16.3	131
Little Rock, AR	49.20	5.4	104
Long Beach, CA	11.54	.1	32
Los Angeles, CA	12.08	.1	36
Louisville, KY	43.56	17.5	125
Madison, WI	30.84	40.8	118
Memphis, TN	51.57	5.5	107
Miami, FL	55.55	0.0	129
Milwaukee, WI	30.94	47.0	125
Minneapolis, MN	26.36	48.9	115
Mobile, AL	64.64	.3	123
Montgomery, AL	49.16	.3	108
Mt. Washington, NH	89.92	246.8	209
Nashville, TN	48.49	11.1	119
Newark, NJ	42.34	28.2	122
New Orleans, LA	59.74	.2	114
New York, NY	42.82	26.1	119
Norfolk, VA	45.22	7.9	115
Oklahoma City, OK	30.89	9.0	82
Olympia, WA	50.96	18.0	164
Omaha, NE	30.34	31.1	98
Philadelphia, PA	41.42	21.9	117
Phoenix, AZ	7.11	.1	36
Pittsburgh, PA	36.30	44.6	154
Portland, ME	43.52	72.4	128
Portland, OR	37.39	6.8	154
Providence, RI	45.32	37.1	124
Raleigh, NC	41.76	7.7	112
Reno, NV	7.49	25.3	51
Richmond, VA	44.07	14.6	113
Russell, NM	9.70	11.4	52
Sacramento, CA	17.10	.1	58
Salt Lake City, UT	15.31	59.1	90
San Antonio, TX	29.13	.4	81
San Diego, CA	9.32	.1	43

San Francisco, CA	19.71	.1	63
Savannah, GA	49.70	.3	111
Seattle, WA	38.60	12.8	158
Sioux Falls, SD	24.12	39.9	96
Spokane, WA	16.71	51.5	114
Springfield, IL	33.78	24.5	114
St. Louis, MO	33.91	19.8	111
Tampa, FL	46.73	.1	107
Toledo, OH	31.78	38.3	137
Tucson, AZ	11.14	1.2	52
Tulsa, OK	38.77	9.0	89
Vero Beach, FL	51.41	0.0	127
Washington, DC	39.00	17.0	112
Wilmington, DE	41.38	20.9	117
Wichita, KA	28.61	16.4	85

GLOSSARY

acid precipitation   Rain or snow with a pH value of less than 5.6.

adibiatic temperature change   A cooling or heating of the air caused by expansion or contraction of air molecules, as opposed to the gain or loss of heat. For example, adiabatic cooling takes place as air rises.

advection   Horizontal movement of air, moisture, or heat.

advection fog   Fog formed by warm, humid air flowing over colder ground or water.

air mass   A large body of air with nearly uniform temperature and moisture content.

airstream   A significant body of air flowing in the same general circulation.

alberta clipper   A small, fast-moving low-pressure system that forms in western Canada and travels southeastward into the United States. These storms, which generally bring little precipitation, generally precede an Arctic air mass.

altitude   Height expressed as the distance above a reference point, which is normally sea level or ground level.

anemometer   An instrument that measures wind speed.

aneroid barometer   An instrument built around a metal structure that bends with changing air pressure. These changes are recorded on a pointer that moves back and forth across a printed scale.

anti-cyclone   A high-pressure system featuring clockwise winds.

Arctic air   A mass of very dry, very cold air that develops over the snow-and-ice-covered regions of the Far North.

atmosphere   The mass of air surrounding the Earth.

atmospheric pressure (also called air pressure or barometric pressure)   The pressure asserted by the mass of the column of air directly above any specific point.

back-door cold front   A cold front that moves in from the northeast, rather than from the normal north or northwest direction.

backing wind   Shifting of the wind in a counterclockwise direction, usually resulting from the approach of a low-pressure system.

barograph   An instrument that provides a continuous record of atmospheric pressure.

barometer An instrument for measuring atmospheric pressure.

barometric tendency The amount and direction of change in barometer readings over a three-hour period.

Beaufort wind scale A system used to classify wind speed, developed in 1805 by British Admiral Francis Beaufort.

biosphere All life on Earth.

blizzard A severe snow storm featuring sustained winds of more than 32 miles per hour, temperatures 10 degrees Fahrenheit or lower, and visibility of 500 feet or less.

ceiling The height above the ground of the base of the lowest layer of clouds, when at least 60 percent of the sky is covered by clouds.

Celsius temperature scale (Also known as Centigrade temperature scale) A temperature scale in which 0 degrees is the melting point of ice and 100 degrees is the boiling point of water.

circulation The pattern of the movement of air. General circulation is the flow of air of large, semi-permanent weather systems, while secondary circulation is the flow of air of more temporary weather systems.

climate A statistical portrait of weather conditions in a specific place over a long period.

climatology The study of climate.

cloudburst A sudden, intense rainfall that is normally of short duration.

cold front The leading edge of a colder mass of air that displaces a warmer mass of air.

condensation The change of vapor to liquid.

condensation nuclei Small particles in the air around which water vapor condenses.

conduction The transfer of heat by molecular action within a substance or when two substances are in direct contact.

continental air mass An air mass that forms over land. It is usually dry, but may be cold or warm.

contrail A cloud-like stream formed in cold, clear air behind the engines of an airplane.

convection The transfer of heat by movement of the heated material. In meteorology, it is often used to indicate the vertical movement of warm air (as opposed to *advection*, the horizontal movement).

Coriolis effect The curving motion of anything, such as air, caused by the rotation of the Earth.

cyclone A low-pressure system in which winds spin inward in a counterclockwise direction in the northern hemisphere.

depression An area of low atmospheric temperature.

dew Water that condenses onto grass and other objects near the ground.

dew point The temperature to which a certain volume of air must be cooled to bring the relative humidity to 100 percent.

disturbance An area of low pressure in which storm conditions occur.

Doppler radar Sophisticated radar that can measure the speed and direction of moving objects, such as wind.

downburst A sudden, strong, downward blast of air, usually from a thundercloud.

drizzle Precipitation featuring tiny water droplets, no more than .02 inches in diameter.

drought Abnormally dry weather in a region over an extended period.

dust devil A small, whirling column of wind that picks up dirt and other loose material as it travels.

equinox The twice-yearly occurrence (about March 21 and September 21) when the sun at its highest point crosses the equator.

extratropical cyclone A cyclone that forms outside of the tropics.

evaporation The change in a substance from a liquid or solid state to a gaseous state.

eye The roughly circular area of relatively calm weather at the center of a hurricane.

Fahrenheit temperature scale A temperature scale that uses 32 degrees as the melting point of ice and 212 degrees as the boiling point of water.

flash flood Flooding caused

by a rapid rise in the water level of rivers, streams, or lakes, usually as a result of heavy rains.

fog A cloud of water droplets suspended in the air that touches the ground.

freezing The change in a substance from a liquid to a solid state.

freezing nuclei Particles suspended in the air around which ice crystals form.

freezing rain Supercooled drops of water that turn to ice when they hit a cold surface.

front The boundary between two different air masses.

frost Ice crystals that form on grass and other objects when the temperature and dew point fall below freezing.

Fujita scale A scale for estimating damage caused by the winds of a tornado, developed by Theodore Fujita.

glaze A smooth coating of ice formed when supercooled water droplets spread out on a surface before freezing.

graupel Precipitation formed when water droplets freeze in layers around a falling ice crystal.

greenhouse effect The warming that takes place when molecules in the atmosphere trap heat radiating away from the surface and redirect it back toward Earth.

Gulf Stream A warm ocean current that flows from the Gulf of Mexico across the Atlantic to the coast of western Europe.

gust A sudden, brief increase in wind speed.

hail Chunks of ice that form in layers in the updrafts of thunderstorms.

halo A ring or arc of light around the sun or moon that is caused by ice crystals in the atmosphere.

haze Particles or fine dust suspended in the air that produce limited visibility.

heat lightning Lightning that can be seen, but is too far away to be heard.

high An area of higher atmospheric pressure.

hurricane A tropical cyclone in the western hemisphere that has sustained wind speeds of 65 miles per hour or greater.

hydrosphere The Earth's water.

hygrometer An instrument that measures the water vapor content of the air.

ice crystals Frozen water vapor suspended in the air.

instability A state of the atmosphere in which convection takes place spontaneously, leading to cloud formation and precipitation.

inversion A condition in which air near the ground is cooler than air above it a condition opposite the normal decrease in temperature with height.

isobar A line on a map that surrounds a mass of air with the same atmospheric pressure.

isotherm A line on a map that surrounds an area with the same temperature.

jet stream A narrow band of winds blowing high in the troposphere at speeds in excess of 57 miles per hour or greater.

Kelvin temperature scale A temperature scale in which 0 degrees is the point at which all molecular motion ceases (absolute zero).

latent heat The energy that is stored when water evaporates. This energy is released when water condenses as a liquid or ice.

lifting The forcing of air in a vertical direction by an upslope in terrain or by the movement of a denser air mass.

lightning An electrical discharge produced by a thunderstorm.

low An area of low atmospheric pressure.

maritime air mass An air mass that forms over water. It is usually humid, and may be cold or warm.

mean temperature The average of a series of temperatures taken over a period of time, such as a day or a month.

mercury barometer An instrument that measures barometric pressure by measuring the level of mercury in a column. An area of low atmospheric pressure.

mesocyclone A large, rotating column of air that forms in a violent thunderstorm and may spawn tornadoes.

microburst A downburst from a thunderstorm that is confined to a small area.

mid-latitudes The areas in

the northern and southern hemispheres between the tropics and the Arctic and Antarctic circles.

millibar A unit of measure of atmospheric pressure.

monsoon A wind that in summer blows from the sea to a continental interior, bringing copious rains.

NEXRAD "Next Generation Weather Radar," a system now being installed across the country by the U.S. Weather Service, the Federal Aviation Administration, and the Department of Defense.

normal A numerical figure representing the average of conditions at a location over a period of years.

numerical forecasting Forecasting the weather through digital computations carried out by supercomputers.

occluded front A boundary between cold and warm air masses that acts like a cold front in some areas and a warm front in others.

orographic lifting The upward flowing of air caused by rising terrain, such as a mountain range.

overrunning The flow of warm air over cold air in advance of a warm front.

ozone An unstable oxygen compound that is a pollutant at ground level, but that absorbs deadly ultraviolet rays in the stratosphere.

ozone hole A thinning of the ozone layer over Antarctica, which occurs each spring.

polar air A mass of very cold, very dry air that forms in polar regions.

precipitation Any liquid or solid form of water that falls from the atmosphere and reaches the surface of the Earth.

pressure gradient force Force acting on air that causes it to move from areas of higher pressure to areas of lower pressure.

prevailing wind The direction from which the wind blows most frequently in any location.

psychrometer An instrument that measures relative humidity of the air.

radar Stands for "radio detection and ranging." An instrument that detects and ranges distant objects by measuring the scattering and reflection of radio beams.

radiation The transferring of energy through electromagnetic waves.

rain Liquid precipitation with drops larger than .02 inches in diameter.

rainbow An arc or circle of colored light caused by the refraction of light by water droplets in the air.

refraction The bending of light as it passes through areas of different density, such as from air through ice crystals.

relative humidity A measure of the amount of water vapor actually held by a specific volume of air in comparison to the maximum water vapor that air could hold at a constant temperature.

ridge An elongated area of high pressure that normally runs north and south.

rime Tiny balls of ice that form when tiny drops of water freeze on contact with the surface.

Saffir-Simpson hurricane damage potential scale A scale that measures hurricane intensity, developed by Herbert Saffir and Robert Simpson.

saturation A condition of the atmosphere in which a certain volume of air holds the maximum water vapor it can hold at a specific temperature.

secondary cold front A front that follows a primary cold front and ushers in even colder air.

shower Snowfall or rainfall of brief duration that can either be heavy or light.

sleet Precipitation consisting of ice particles formed when raindrops freeze.

smog Air pollution caused by a mixture of smoke and fog.

snow Precipitation consisting of clumps of ice crystals.

solar energy The energy produced by the sun.

solstice The time of year when the sun is the farthest north or the farthest south (about June 21 and December 21).

squall line A line of thunderstorms that forms along a front.

stable air Air in which temperature and humidity at various levels discourage the formation of convection currents.

stationary front The border between cold and warm air

masses that are not moving.

storm track The path that storms generally follow in a given area.

sublimation The change of water vapor directly into ice crystals or ice crystals directly into water vapor.

supercell thunderstorm An unusually violent thunderstorm that is capable of generating tornadoes.

subsidence The descent of a body of air, usually in a high-pressure area, that warms the lower levels of air.

supercooled water Water cooled to a temperature of less than 32 degrees Fahrenheit without freezing.

thermometer An instrument for measuring temperature.

temperate zone The area of the globe between the tropics and the polar regions.

thunder The sound produced by lightning discharges.

thunderstorms Storms that produce lightning and thunder.

tornado A violently rotating column of air that reaches from the base of a cloud to the ground.

tropics The area of the globe from latitudes 23.5 degrees north to 23.5 degrees south.

tropical air Warm, humid air masses that form in tropical regions.

tropical cyclone A low-pressure system that forms in the tropics.

tropical depression A tropical cyclone with winds of less than 30 miles per hour.

tropical storm A tropical cyclone with winds of 31 to 74 miles per hour.

trough An elongated low-pressure system that generally stretches north and south.

typhoon A tropical cyclone with winds of 75 miles per hour or greater that occurs west of the International Date Line.

unstable air Air with temperature differences that encourage the formation of convection currents that can produce clouds and precipitation.

updraft An upward current of air, usually within a thundercloud.

veering winds Winds that shift in a clockwise direction, a shift caused by a high-pressure system.

visibility The greatest distance at which one can see and identify objects.

virga Water droplets or ice crystals that fall from high clouds but that evaporate before hitting the ground.

warm front The leading edge of a mass of warmer air that displaces a mass of colder air.

water vapor The invisible gaseous form of water.

wave A small cyclonic circulation in the early stages of development that moves along a cold front.

weather The conditions in the atmosphere at any given time.

wind Air in motion that moves relatively horizontally in relationship to the surface of the Earth.

windchill factor A measure of the effect of wind in increasing the heat loss from exposed flesh.

wind direction The direction from which the wind is blowing.

wind shear A sudden shift in wind direction.

INDEX